Making News in the Digital Era

Making News in the Digital Era

DAVID E. HENDERSON

iUniverse, Inc.
New York   Bloomington

Making News in the Digital Era

Copyright © 2009 David E. Henderson

All rights reserved. No part of this book may be used or reproduced by any means, graphic, electronic, or mechanical, including photocopying, recording, taping or by any information storage retrieval system without the written permission of the publisher except in the case of brief quotations embodied in critical articles and reviews.

The views expressed in this work are solely those of the author and do not necessarily reflect the views of the publisher, and the publisher hereby disclaims any responsibility for them.

iUniverse books may be ordered through booksellers or by contacting:

iUniverse
1663 Liberty Drive
Bloomington, IN 47403
www.iuniverse.com
1-800-Authors (1-800-288-4677)

Because of the dynamic nature of the Internet, any Web addresses or links contained in this book may have changed since publication and may no longer be valid. The views expressed in this work are solely those of the author and do not necessarily reflect the views of the publisher, and the publisher hereby disclaims any responsibility for them.

ISBN: 978-1-4401-5307-5 (pbk)
ISBN: 978-1-4401-5306-8 (cloth)
ISBN: 978-1-4401-5308-2 (ebk)

Cover design by TM Design, Inc.
Author photo by Ed Lallo

Printed in the United States of America

iUniverse rev. date: 9/10/2009

For Kit

And to Val Fex

Contents

Introduction ix

Part 1. Torrents of Change.

Chapter One:	Everything Is Upside Down 3
Chapter Two:	Bright Stars and Clear Voices 10
Chapter Three:	Leadership in the Digital Revolution 18
Chapter Four:	Creating Symbolic Images 28
Chapter Five:	Take Charge of Your Own Success 30
Chapter Six:	Road Map of the New Online World 36
Chapter Seven:	Twitter Dispatches in 140 Characters 43
Chapter Eight:	Find Something That Works 51
Chapter Nine:	Blogging Has Come a Long Way 59
Chapter Ten:	Untangling Online Strategies and Web 2.0 .. 68

Part 2. Get in the Game. Make a Difference.

Chapter Eleven:	Each of Us Has a Voice 75
Chapter Twelve:	Communications with Impact 79
Chapter Thirteen:	Crisis Never Takes a Day Off 82
Chapter Fourteen:	Working in the World's Spotlight 85
Chapter Fifteen:	Awareness That Saves Lives 93

Part 3. Reaching. Engaging. Influencing.

Chapter Sixteen:	A Good Story Has Great Legs 103
Chapter Seventeen:	Perception Is Just Reality's Mirror Image ... 109
Chapter Eighteen:	Plain Language Is Sexy 112
Chapter Nineteen:	Die, Press Releases! 117

Chapter Twenty:	Nothing Is Secret, or "No Comment"	122
Chapter Twenty-One:	Strategic Planning While You Wait	128
Chapter Twenty-Two:	Mission Statements Are Useless	134
Chapter Twenty-Three:	The Price of a Forgettable Slogan	141
Chapter Twenty-Four:	A Handshake Rather Than E-Mail	147
Chapter Twenty-Five:	Be Clever and Bold	152
Chapter Twenty-Six:	Ready for 15 Minutes	158
Chapter Twenty-Seven:	The Camera Never Blinks	163
Chapter Twenty-Eight:	Core Values and Clear Vision	166

Introduction

It used to be said that mainstream media was the world's most powerful form of mass communication. It was a world of paper by the ton, ink by the gallon and major network news ruling the airwaves. That was true, once upon a time.

Before the Internet, organizations had to communicate to their audiences primarily through the traditional media as the mouthpiece, and it was sometimes a challenge.

The list of how mainstream media has impacted our world and our lives is long, and its power has been ubiquitous. But times are changing.

Twitter This

Fast forward to now … and Twitter this: The online democratization of mass communications is redefining how people connect, businesses work and governments run. (Incidentally, that sentence is written to conform to Twitter's allowed 140-character limit.)

Result: There's a bit of mass hysteria among the mass media as they turn themselves inside out trying to make sense and money out of this quicksilver technology "of the people, by the people and for the people."

Google "Abraham Lincoln," who spoke those words, and see if the wise man saw this coming. Few did.

Digitally Driven

We are currently experiencing an information revolution that's digitally driven, ones and zeros, in a new-world business matrix and model. Organizations — large and small, no name or brand name, legitimate or outlaw — can simply bypass mainstream media to communicate *their* news, *their* way, directly and effectively, to *their* publics. They can pick *their* media: Web sites, blogs, YouTube videos, and online sharing and social networking sites.

Those are some of the obvious choices. Lord only knows what new look-at-me technology awaits our next click of the computer mouse.

We live in a communications world where new and not-so-new ways collide, merge and morph, all with the intent to better connect with our audiences. What we must do is identify and capitalize on the best of new trends to meet specific objectives, tap into all the new methods to build awareness that will be described in this book, shape the news to our best advantage and profit from the results. So, I ask you:

- Do you want your organization to be heard above competitors' noise?

- Do you want to capture this new media's attention when the time is right?

- Do you want to increase the "Googleability" of your organization?

- Do you want to have more meaningful conversations with key stakeholders and audiences?

If so, then read on. But prepare yourself to think, engage and strike out in bold new directions.

Given the "e-ness" of it all, the days when businesses or organizations needed mainstay public relations agencies to reach their audiences are disappearing fast. Today, any organization linked up with a few smart resources can create and deliver targeted, sophisticated communications without needing full-blown agencies.

It is little surprise that businesses, organizations, politicians and others appreciate and covet new communications techniques and channels for getting their points of view out there in the world, without someone else's filter or interpretation. Quite simply, the status is no longer quo in the scramble for competitive leadership.

The "Me" in Media

The style of discourse has changed to engagement, interactions, listening and, ultimately, immediate and transparent online conversations. Audiences do not care to hear an organization talk about itself. People only want to know how an organization's products or services benefit them and bring value to their lives. It's all about the "me" in this new-day *me*dia.

Given the shifting landscape, mainstream media now struggles to reinvent itself while its online counterparts evolve at dizzying speeds. Think of it as digital Darwinism. For us who make a living through communications, the challenge becomes keeping pace — if not setting the pace — to serve our organizations, clients and ourselves in relevant and responsible ways.

For many agencies and PR departments, however, change is either too slow in coming or is not happening. There's a communications tsunami rolling our way, and many of us are not sure what to do. Sure, we see the tide going out fast and far. It's fascinating and scary at the same time. Standing on the beach and waiting for it to roar back in is not an option.

Get to High Ground

So how do we get to high ground that's well above the communications storm surge?

This book gives you practical ways to communicate in our world today, where century-old institutions like major dailies are dying one by one as rewarding online opportunities appear and prosper.

It is written for businesspeople, communications professionals, PR agencies, nongovernmental entities and not-for-profit organizations. This book is intended to present an integrated approach to communications in the online era, delivering value in the form of awareness, influence, differentiation and that ever-so-elusive competitive advantage.

The following chapters are for anyone who wants to become an authentic communications leader in the digital era. Readers will find useful insight into new techniques for connecting with audiences and making news — for themselves and the organizations they represent.

Controlling the Conversation

Over my career as a CBS News journalist, and then in the 25-plus years as a strategic communications executive, I cannot begin to name all the chief executives who demanded great media coverage but responded with disdain at any suggestion of speaking with reporters. They didn't trust the media, belittled reporters and treated any interaction with them as an intrusion. They expected great media coverage, and heads would roll if they didn't get it. Yet does this type of executive fully know what the media has become today?

And why is that?

The chance of newspaper coverage may no longer exist if the paper itself is no longer in business, replaced by local ad hoc news blogs.

In the mainstream media, those chief executives could never control the conversation. With the Internet, if they get involved and have their own designated sites and spaces, whether blogs or otherwise, their voices can now be heard unfiltered, and their stories told in full, if that's their desire.

Of course, this freedom of corporate expression ushers in new forces as well, both friend and foe, which brings us back to the "me" in this new era of media.

Look in the Mirror

Who is the media today? Just look in the mirror. It's all of us. The Internet has altered the definition of the very word and has enabled everyone, from everywhere, to have his or her opinions known. Of course, such a land rush of opportunity attracts all kinds, professionals and amateurs alike, some with bona fide credentials and some with only self-promoting expertise.

Be they pro or punk, there is nowhere to hide from them in the media now owned by the masses in the digital era.

An executive who avoids or dismisses the new trends defining media, today and into the future, who denies his or her key publics and refuses to personally engage in communicating a corporate or business vision is placing the organization's potential for competitive growth and prosperity at risk.

Any PR agency or corporate communications shop that does not learn and embrace the more fluid, timely and relevant methods for effective communications in the digital era will be hitting the DELETE button on their futures. Many PR agencies already are obsolete; they just don't know it yet.

The book you are holding presents practical, easy and fast techniques for strategic communications planning, which will achieve the awareness, influence and results you desire. In addition, you will learn how to use the outreach tactics or tools available with Web 2.0 to create near-instantaneous results.

David E. Henderson

PART 1
Torrents of Change.

Chapter One:
Everything Is Upside Down

We are inundated today by marketing and promotional message clutter, which is driven by fierce competition among businesses, organizations and individuals with agendas — all vying for attention. In this digital age, it seems as if we are in a world of high-intensity information overload. We attempt to tune out much of the noise, yet many of us remain captivated by the clever, credible and original.

The online environment is new for many organizations desiring to create attention and have their messages heard. Resisting or rejecting contemporary ideas for communications means risking being lost in the shadows and dust. It is a time when better techniques are needed to boost awareness and reach objectives.

The challenge is how to successfully achieve meaningful results through effectively and credibly connecting with audiences and, in particular, the media, both mainstream and online. The goals for a business or organization may include growth, enhanced image and reputation before key audiences, increased financial security and being recognized as a leader.

We are living in the online era, a fact that cannot be avoided. There are approximately 199.2 million Internet users in the United States, according to eMarketer.[1] Two out of every three people in the country are actively online.

Organizations can no longer afford to cling to old-school tactics and hope to succeed. It is a new era, in when reaching objectives and success is equated to management of prominent awareness, engagement with audiences and effective competitive differentiation.

---

[1] http://www.emarketer.com

It has become a bewildering world, filled with noise, clutter and change, especially in how we communicate and how we scramble to get the attention of the media. The methods of our conversations are evolving; the style of discourse is changing. How we get our news, are informed and share information is changing as well. Even those we have conversations with have changed, as we sometimes share with and learn from people we may never meet in person.

In our own organizations, we want to be clear, decisive and efficient leaders, managers and communicators. But then things get complicated. We know what we want to say, and we want to act quickly, but since many people need to be involved in the approval process, we have numerous meetings to make sure we have covered everything. And time passes even as the rest of the world races by. Many of our efforts to communicate are held back by rigid internal processes and politics, as well as inflexible old habits.

In the media, an entire industry that clung too long to old business models and old habits is changing and dying before our eyes. The newspaper business as it has traditionally been known is crumbling as advertising dollars and readers have swarmed to the efficiency and instant convenience of the Internet. The definitions of what is news and who is a journalist are swiftly being altered.

Every week, if not every day, we hear of more newspapers failing or struggling to stay alive. Newsrooms are cutting staffs, cutting sections, cutting pages. Some of the best newspeople in the business have lost their jobs. The industry has been trying to find a silver bullet, a new business model, to attract more readers and larger revenue streams online. It has not had much luck so far. The traditional American press is on suicide watch.

Frank Rich, a respected columnist at the *New York Times*, pulled no punches about the situation of traditional media when he observed in a May 10, 2009, *Times* column: "Newspaper circulations and revenues are in free fall ... [and] the reporting ranks on network and local [TV] news alike are shriveling."

Rich continued: "The causes of journalism's downfall — some self-inflicted, some beyond anyone's control (a worldwide economic meltdown) — are well known." He characterized it as "self-destructive retreat from innovation."

With the advent of new forms of media, made possible by the online digital revolution, we seemingly have infinite avenues to find news and information at our fingertips, and we can explore new ways of having our voices heard. We care less today about what someone is pushing at us and more about our own personal choices — a trend that has turned the whole world of marketing and advertising upside down.

The big advantage is that today we can do something about it. We all can be actively a part of the online discourse to have our voices, news and information heard and seen. It only takes learning the new ways to work in the digital era.

Just as we in the communications industry would no longer consider sending a news release to the media in the mail or via fax, for example, we must also question the relevance of even using such things as news releases and other more traditional communication tactics.

With downsizing of mainstream media, those journalists who still have jobs are under increased pressure to find new and clever stories that have not appeared elsewhere. Why, then, would they consider a press release? Nonetheless, the PR industry — clinging staunchly to its old-school ways — continues to send out thousands of press releases, most of which are never read.

The harsh truth today is that nobody cares when an organization talks about itself. Today's publics, or a company's particular audiences, only care how they benefit from an organization's products or services.

The old style of advertising and marketing is changing before our eyes as revolutionary new creative methods, which are more efficient and cost less, take shape, usually online. The idea of big, pricey Madison Avenue-type advertising agencies is becoming obsolete.

The days of massive spending on advertising campaigns to debut new products or ideas are waning. Generating influence requires clever exposure across the diverse and evolving channels of the traditional news media, together with a savvy use of the new spectrum of digital media, including blogs, podcasts, social networking, streaming video and engaging people in conversations online. An imaginative one-minute video on YouTube that was made on a shoestring budget has the potential today of being viewed by millions of people and delivering substantial results.

There are already warning signs that the traditional model of many public relations agencies that embraces hourly billing, and tactics that have not changed in decades, is headed for trouble. In the digital age, it is possible for any individuals or organizations to manage their own communications outreach efficiently, relying on assistance from specialists and consultants, without the need for a full-blown PR agency.

It is no surprise, then, that corporations and organizations, including the big public relations agencies, are scrambling to understand how to communicate in the complex digital world of instantaneous deadlines, where all the rules are changing. Even the tactical steps of how to connect with journalists and bloggers, as well as the burgeoning popularity of online interactivity and social media communities, are new.

There has been a flurry of excitement over the exciting new tools of the digital revolution. Should an organization or CEO have a blog? How about podcasts and streaming video? What are the merits of a special wiki to explain a technical industry or complex issues? What about the plethora of online services that promises to deliver your press release into the hands of thousands of reporters?

How do you make intelligent choices about what works to attract attention and what does not? We must begin by stepping back and taking a more strategic and realistic view of the competitive landscape. Put aside for a moment all the tactical choices for things like interactive sites, streaming video, viral word-of-mouth tactics, social networks, branding in a virtual world, online newsrooms, blogs and so on in order to focus on understanding far more important dynamics: What's driving interest in the digital environment?

Here's a reality: The ability to inspire and communicate passion, value and clear purpose to achieve solid results in today's digital revolution is always strategically driven. It begins with a clear vision of a business or organization's core purpose and developing a credible, authentic voice.

What's an organization's authentic overarching story that will stop audiences in their tracks, to listen and engage? Strategic purpose today focuses on who you are, rather than who you say you are.

It comes alive by having a clear grasp of both the established techniques of communications and the evolving world of both mainstream media, as well as a dizzying array of new communications methods online. An effective communicator today must know how to work in both worlds of communications with a firm grasp of trends, protocols, ethics and opportunities.

Effective and responsible awareness leadership, the kind that delivers the results you desire, is an imperfect, evolving craft at best, and it can be extremely powerful.

The practice of influential communications with the media comes from realistic knowledge of what makes appealing news, what is and is not a story identifying the best news outlet to reach your audiences, finding a reporter who agrees with you about the story, and working with the reporter to develop a story with which you will be pleased. The goal is to reach and engage audiences.

What Starbucks pulled off in May 2009 is a good example of comprehensively using traditional and online media. The coffeehouse chain wanted to tell its message to a new generation of coffee drinkers and encourage them to retell the story online.

Starbucks put up large advertising posters in six major cities. To build awareness, it turned to popular online social media sites, including Twitter and Facebook, and challenged people to find the location of each poster, snap a photo and post it on Twitter.

Faced with competition from other food chains, including McDonald's and Dunkin' Donuts, Starbucks issued this promise in the poster advertisements: "If your coffee isn't perfect, we'll make it over. If it's still not perfect, you must not be in a Starbucks."

Not only did the Starbucks campaign generate considerable buzz online, but it also captured significant mainstream media attention, including a half-page story in the business section of the *New York Times*.

Because of the near-instant credibility and widespread audience reach that comes with news coverage, media outreach — traditional and online — can be the most influential tool in an organization's marketing strategy. You can boost brand awareness for an organization, prominently position a product or service, attract new customers, provide clear and accurate information in a crisis, and help to right a wrong, among other desired results.

In the field of public relations and communications, it used to be that we just had to keep track of mainstream journalists — those who worked at newspapers, wire services, magazines, radio and television — as they moved around their industry or within their organizations. Today, as communicators, we have more formidable challenges to tackle.

In my experience in the field of strategic communications, I have identified six strategic top-level action items for today's communicator to consider. I have found that these serve as a beacon for lighting a meaningful path to success:

- Advocate change: Learn the styles, trends and new protocols of today's mainstream and online media as it shifts and jockeys to find a niche. Champion change in your own organization. Old habits die hard at many organizations, slowing them from learning new styles and embracing new techniques. While it might be an old habit and more comfortable, for example, to send out a press release, that kind of outreach has become less effective in today's competitive world.

- Embrace storytelling: Learn how to tell what your organization has to say in an appealing story. Forget slogans, marketing lingo and advertising catch phrases. Storytelling is an astonishingly influential technique for any organization or business to attract attention and trigger word-of-mouth buzz that will ultimately enhance leadership positioning. The media, whether mainstream or online, is always looking for a good story.

- Use plain language: The communications clarity of business and organizations is too often polluted by obfuscated language of industry shorthand or overworked business school jargon. As a communicator, translate opaque into plain and clear language that everyone will understand.

- Reach out to few to achieve more: Develop working relationships with those individuals — whether journalists, bloggers, analysts or others — whose opinions tend to influence others in your industry or business sector. Chances are, the list of authentic influencers is astonishingly short. In technology's consumer products area, for example, David Pogue of the *New York Times* and Walt Mossberg of the *Wall Street Leader* are the primary thought leaders. What they write and say often influences what the rest of the media reports. (Note that there are influential people like Pogue and Mossberg in every industry and field of expertise.) Aside from promoting your own organization, strive to become a valued and trusted resource to such thought leaders in the media. The days of blasting out press releases to thousands of people are quickly coming to an end for the simple reason that a release sent to everyone is the antithesis of what any journalist wants or needs for a story in today's media environment.

- Stop marketing and promoting; start listening: We are living and working in a new world influenced by vast choices online, a world of diminished influence for traditional advertising, marketing and promotion. This is the hardest thing for many organizations to grasp. We must let go of old ways, listen to the people who matter most to our organizations — customers, clients, buyers, stakeholders, the media — and get into conversations with all of them. There's an old belief that the best kind of promotion is when an influential thought leader says something nice about you, and it's never been truer than today. Listening and conversations lead to those who matter most to your organization telling others nice things about you. They become an army of ambassadors who are on your side, which can enhance the best kind of awareness.

- Become the credible voice and face of your organization and industry: Look around at today's most respected organizations. In many cases, the top executives have high visibility and are recognized as leaders with near-celebrity status. They define and differentiate the image, integrity and reputation of their organizations through their own consistent openness and transparency as industry leaders, often leaving less outward CEOs to stand in the shadows.

It is not that difficult to achieve organizational image leadership and a clear voice to capitalize on all the communications opportunities around us. It begins with the discipline of letting go of old habits that often no longer work, recognizing that if we do not get more savvy as communicators, we might wake up someday to find that our competitors have.

Chapter Two:
Bright Stars and Clear Voices

There are important voices that gain trust and change how business is done worldwide. We hear the voices of these highly successful leaders and executives who use the awesome power of the media, online and mainstream, to build trust in the brand value of their corporations, activist groups, associations and nongovernmental organizations.

During the course of researching this book, I spoke with many bloggers, journalists and visionaries in the field of communications. They shared their opinions about today's most interesting executives, providing an insider's perspective on the latest trends in communications. I also interviewed outstanding leaders of corporations, nonprofits and associations who are recognized for being credible, transparent and effective communicators.

A few select yet exceptionally influential executives generate media coverage that is usually reserved for rock stars, only this group is far more grounded and credible. It includes such people as Steve Jobs, Oprah Winfrey, Layli Miller-Muro, Tony Hsieh and Sir Richard Branson. They know how to enhance their own images, worth and the way we view and respect them as leaders.

The list of people who authentically respect the value of a clear, influential voice is exclusive and astonishingly short, in fact, which begs the question: How do *these* people enrapture audiences, capture the attention of reporters and command such enormous coverage?

Tony Hsieh is the popular founder and CEO of Zappos, the phenomenally successful online shoe store. He is in the news frequently, and you will read more about him later in this book.

You may not recognize Ms. Miller-Muro's name among Branson, Jobs, Oprah or the others, but she is clearly a leading communicator in the not-for-profit world, as I will also explain a little later.

These leaders all share common threads of skill as great communicators, including the exceptional ability to get to the point — quickly, clearly and in simple words — so that we stop what we are doing to listen, understand and believe what they say.

These savvy few also know that successful image leadership requires accepting responsibility for managing reputation, involvement in strategic communications planning, the integration of communications throughout all levels of their organizations, and their own engagement in behaving as an authentic leader.

The people at the top must be involved and accountable. Why? Because too much is at stake. The value of managing an organization's reputation in today's digital environment is too important to be delegated.

Amid all the competitive clutter or noise in a marketplace, many CEOs and academics see an organization's reputation as merely a perception, impression or intangible *feeling* that people have about their brands. As such, a reputation is fragile and must be managed.

While he is a private person, let's take a closer look at the public style of one of the world's most effective business communicators, Steve Jobs.

Jobs, the legendary cofounder and head of Apple, is an icon in the business of technology, and I will write about him throughout this book as an example of someone who truly understands how to make news in the digital era.

When Jobs speaks before any audience, he has a cultivated gift for distilling and translating highly technical concepts and issues into simple, easy-to-understand and memorable statements and stories.

In an industry where so many people have a natural impulse to "talk tech," Jobs takes a different approach: He shares new ideas and his passion for what Apple creates in plain, familiar language, even when he is talking with reporters who cover the technology business.

Why? Well, it is quite simple. Jobs knows and respects the role of reporters and bloggers as conduits who will carry his words and perspective about new products and industry developments to much broader audiences, including you and me. He also knows there is nothing to be gained by talking over our heads.

Jobs communicates clearly and masterfully on an individual basis with bloggers and reporters, whether a roomful or just a few. People who cover the news and write stories — through the news organizations or blogs they represent — wield influence to carry forward the image of charisma, leadership and excitement in his words.

Jobs's persuasiveness stems from his personal certainty in his beliefs. When he speaks of an Apple product, for example, you begin to believe that it is the greatest device ever created because Steve Jobs believes it is so. His transparency may seem like a crippling liability, but it is actually a strength.

Here's a technique used by visionaries like Jobs: The genuine core messages of today's most effective communicators are interwoven throughout all levels of their organizations to enhance understanding, excitement in the company's mission, respect for the intelligence of leadership and, ultimately, the brand image and reputation. It is like a beacon that clarifies understanding and builds consensus. It's also a story that people find so appealing that it is repeated — over and over and over — further extending a good image and reputation of an executive and organization.

When Jobs makes a statement, everyone at Apple — from salespeople in retail outlets worldwide, to technical and customer support experts at call centers — not only learns the news at near-light speed, but also comprehends his vision and passion, as well as how they translate into the company's unique style. Not surprisingly, the brightness of their enthusiasm shines from within the company and helps Jobs inspire the world.

An effective media strategy may begin with a terrific coverage angle that gets our attention, but that's only part of a contemporary strategic approach to communications. As mentioned previously, an authentic leader's interface with the media must be reflected throughout the organization's promotion and marketing matrix. Each dynamic of the leader's vision is told, retold and threaded seamlessly into the organization's communications — online Web sites and media, traditional media, broadcast radio and television, streaming video, podcasts, in-store displays, posters, blogs and advertising materials.

Even the style by which employees interact personally with stakeholders, customers, vendors and people who are just window-shopping should be seamlessly woven into communications. This holistic approach involves audiences, increases impact, controls favorable perceptions and delivers successful results. Such a style even reaches and excites the financial crowd and shareholders on Wall Street.

It all begins with a captivating story that is communicated by the person at the top, a story that then trickles down and excites the entire organization and is repeated.

What makes a keynote address or news conference by Steve Jobs so compelling is that his opinions translate directly into Apple's policies and products. Jobs consistently demonstrates his extraordinary merging of unique management and communication styles.

No one person, not even a visionary CEO like Jobs, can control every detail of every product, but Jobs has proven his willingness to reach all the way down the organizational chart and make decisions about even the smallest features, according to people close to the company. His readiness to roll up his shirtsleeves and exert control and leadership over anything makes the legendary idea that he controls *everything* seem, well, reasonable.

As one Jobs observer noted to me, "His tendency to micromanage can more charitably be viewed as a refreshing willingness to cut through bureaucracy. Few 'insanely great' products are created by committees, after all."

Jobs's leadership style is a dramatic change from the traditional leadership style at most organizations, which seems haphazard or lame by comparison. Few executives invest significant time and energy venturing into the dusty corners of their organizations to inspire greatness. Even fewer work to avoid bureaucracy. When it comes to communicating messages, the traditional and commonly accepted attempts to get media attention — for example, by distributing prepared and sterile-sounding statements that have been edited and scrubbed by attorneys, department heads, supervisors and PR people — and their associated results often are disappointing. They simply are not in the same class as companies like Apple.

Another reason today's great communicators are so successful is that their messages are transparent, truthful, timely and consistent.

"Sixteen years on *Face the Nation* has taught me one thing," CBS newsman Bob Schieffer told me. "When I ask a question and guests start laying out conditions such as 'First let me tell you,' or, 'The real questions is,' or, 'It is important to put that in context,' I know we're headed down the old rabbit trail that will take us anywhere but to a straight answer.

"When people want to answer, they do so quickly, directly and clearly," he said. "When they don't, we get all those conditions and lectures about the importance of context. I've been dragged down that old rabbit trail too many times by too many people with something to hide."

Schieffer was saying that he expects truth and straight answers, without equivocation, when he asks a question of a newsmaker — no stalling or dancing away from the subject. Don't we all?

Of course, what Schieffer expects from a newsmaker and what he gets are not always the same thing.

What it boils down to is that an investment to protect a reputation is infinitely less than the expense needed to fix one that is damaged, sometimes by self-inflicted mistakes.

Dr. Paul A. Argenti at Dartmouth University's Tuck School of Business has written, "Risks to reputation can be among the most damaging a company can face. But because they are often intangible, they can also be extremely difficult to manage."

I contacted Argenti at Dartmouth to learn more about a survey conducted by the public relations firm Hill & Knowlton and recruiters Korn/Ferry, in which he cites that of 200 companies, nearly two-thirds of CEOs worldwide say it is their personal responsibility to manage the company's reputation.

"Although most senior executives would agree that reputation is important," Argenti explained, "no single person or position is ultimately responsible for managing reputation and assessing its risk on a day-to-day basis. As a result, before it can even begin to defend or regain momentum, the organization inevitably burns up valuable time and opportunity in an internal struggle to reach a consensus about the state of its reputation."

Top executives, leaders and professional communicators who have taken the time, as leaders in their respective fields, understand how the media works. As newsmakers, they know what to say and how to deliver their messages so that reporters will pay attention and will most often write positive stories.

Such leaders know that reporters look for sound bites and quotable quotes — not lengthy explanations — so they get to their point quickly when communicating their messages. They concisely and clearly articulate the vision of their respective organizations in a way that excites people and creates positive results.

Although these executives have support staff, they have not delegated the voice of their organizations to others. They not only deliver communications but also put a face on their organizations. As a public and an audience, we immediately recognize these leaders and trust what they say.

During my many years in the consulting business, I have seen all kinds of top executives. A good many may talk about the importance of building a good brand image and reputation, yet few actually step up to the plate to invest the necessary time to set the course and make their vision successful.

It's not realistic, I know, for top executives to micromanage image outreach efforts, unless you are Apple's Steve Jobs. But someone at the top must be accountable and take ownership for a communications initiative that underscores an organization's transparency, openness and clarity, especially in today's competitive digital environment.

The respect and trust of any business or organization is too important for any CEO or top manager to delegate to someone else, even though we've seen it happen many times. When responsibility is delegated, focus of vision invariably is diluted, misinterpreted, confused and/or gets lost in the weeds.

Captivating leaders, by contrast, know that in today's highly competitive world, successful endeavors become even more successful when they reflect the personality and charisma of the person at the helm. They also know that the way that person behaves in the public spotlight is key.

While Sir Richard Branson does not run all the estimated 350 companies under his Virgin brand, his individual image and voice is what brings each of them to life. With the magnificent grace and timing of a symphony conductor, Branson captures terrific and consistent media coverage. Audiences on every continent love and trust him.

Oprah Winfrey is unique. She is the brand, the product, the center of her successful universe and its singular voice to the public. Everything is all about Oprah, all the time — from Oprah's book club to her magazine to her programs to build schools.

Winfrey's strategic formula is genuine, connects passionately with a sizable loyal audience and works to make things happen. She often creates her own news, always in a manner that embraces her fans and respects the projects to which she lends her name. When not communicated through her own media channels, including a news magazine-style Web site and *O, The Oprah Magazine*, Winfrey's stories pull the mainstream news media like a magnet, due in large measure to her celebrity.

Few successfully identify the magic key to unlock access to the world of Oprah and attract her interest. But Oprah's endorsement is golden. Thousands of people go knocking on her door, yet only a few actually get to stand in the warm spotlight with her.

Leaders like Jobs and Winfrey know that the power of reaching out and engaging large audiences is frequently accessed through credible and popular appeal of media coverage, both mainstream and online. They are also aware that the influence of traditional advertising in today's world has been greatly diminished, partly due to all the media choices at our fingertips and the competitive clutter created by the confluence of traditional and evolving online media.

So, what do today's most influential leaders have in common? Storytelling is one shared trait. The use of clear, plain language is another.

Today's successful leaders have the skills to communicate corporate messages and unique perspectives through ordinary words and clever stories that capture our attention, involve us in what seems like exclusive insight into their vision for the future, and motivate us to action. Outstanding leaders attract our attention or generate great news coverage because they give us, and they give journalists, exactly what we desire: a compelling story.

Watch these leaders closely. While in the media's glare, they introduce new products, services or ideas by sharing captivating stories. They speak in quotable quotes — a few short, appealing words that are precisely the sort of thing that reporters listen for and, in fact, need to develop stories.

We watch, listen, read and get excited about their messages because these leaders share their stories with *us*. They make us feel special, and we view them as authentic leaders of the best kind.

Influential leaders get right to the point and explain about often-complex issues in simple terms so we all can understand. After all, they are sharing stories that excite them; we can sense and share in their enthusiasm and passion. They are not afraid of having a sense of humor, showing humility or being human. We admire them, relate to them and believe we understand what they are saying. In most cases, our positive perception of the companies or organizations they lead increases.

Most of all, such leaders accept responsibility and accountability. We and the media trust them and the brands they represent.

In addition to their authentic storytelling ability, these leaders also share an understanding that in today's world, which is full of shouted marketing promotions, hype and message clutter, they need to get to the point clearly and quickly when they have something to say. Plain language consists of words that everyone understands and is free of jargon, cliques, acronyms and gobbledygook.

The stories effective leaders present are structured like a pyramid, with a point on top. That's important because in today's world, which is filled with noise and competitive clutter, we need to immediately get to the point of what we are saying.

Think about the image of a pyramid, a shape that expands from the top downward to a broad base. When speaking with audiences or reporters, get to the point first, and then provide greater understanding through anecdotes, facts and examples. That is the best approach. It doesn't hurt to make our stories short, sweet and framed to appeal to logic, common sense and emotion.

Through stories, we can credibly communicate important yet intangible issues, such as why the audience should value or care about a product, service or cause. We can subtly position ourselves as a trusted partner to share a vision or quest with an audience and, in the process, achieve lasting competitive leadership.

The benefits of using storytelling will seemingly happen automatically — a closer connection with audiences, enhanced trust and a reputation for candor, openness and transparency — and they will result in quicker and more favorable results.

Chapter Three:
Leadership in the Digital Revolution

Billionaire entrepreneur Mark Cuban makes clear the importance of knowing how to use the Internet to communicate, to engage in conversations with audiences and to build brand awareness and value. Cuban is owner of HDNet, the high-definition cable television network, and the Dallas Mavericks, among other ventures.

The Internet has been an essential communication tool for Cuban's business empire. As a high-profile executive, he's actively online and in touch through his personal blog, Blog Maverick.[2]

"In the Internet age," Cuban told me during an e-mail interview, "executives have to learn how to shape information about themselves and their companies, or the Internet will do it for them, and it won't be pretty."

The once-effective support structure for executives and leaders — such as public relations, marketing and advertising agencies — has been shockingly slow to learn the new and ever-changing trends of how to use the Internet. Conventional methods of getting an organization's messages communicated with key audiences directly and through the traditional mainstream media are either broken or less effective.

It is up to an executive or communicator, according to Cuban, to take the initiative and responsibility to get smart about the Internet and the new ways of communicating in today's online world at a time when there is chaos within the mainstream media.

It's being said within the news industry that the traditional media gatekeepers — publishers, editors, producers and other people who

---

[2] www.blogmaverick.com

decided what was or was not *news* — no longer have any gates to keep. The situation is clearly that stark, and worse.

The news industry is undergoing a major decline, driven by a massive slump in profits at news organizations, shifts in advertising dollars, changes in consumer interests and new forms of engaging audiences online. The evolving online technology is attracting larger and younger audiences, and not many of them are interested in media tradition.

Multiple surveys, including those by the Pew Research Center, reveal similar trends: We prefer to get our news and information from free online sources rather than picking up a newspaper or switching on the evening TV newscasts.

In a near-desperate attempt to attract readers and viewers, mainstream print and television media is reaching out to audiences and asking us to share photos or video of news that we see. We have all become the media, in one form or another, for we are "citizen journalists."

What mainstream media has failed to recognize is that many of us have been citizen journalists for years, through blogs and other online information-sharing sites.

National Public Radio's Juan Williams summed it up best when he told me, "We live in times of national discontent and tremendous change — political, among demographics, and within our society."

Within that environment, he said, the media is struggling to reinvent itself, connect with audiences and give their audiences what they want and expect to hear.

During consulting, strategic communications workshops and lectures, I have been asked questions about new trends and challenges in working with an ever-changing news media. What works, and what is no longer effective? How do I communicate with reporters, bloggers and all my key audiences? What is the definition of "journalist" in today's world of online citizen reporters? How beneficial is online technology for strategic communications — like interactive sites, streaming video, viral word-of-mouth tactics, social media, Web site newsrooms and blogs — and what are just passing fads? What new tools of strategic communications are viable? What's the future of video news releases? How about the effectiveness of traditional media kits, news conferences and news releases?

In a panic attack, many in the public relations industry are scrambling to embrace the elements of the online media world. WAKE UP TO NEW MEDIA OR LOSE CLIENTS screamed a trade newsletter headline. Many others in the PR business are on the trailing edge of the trend, if at all.

Within many public relations agencies of all sizes, there remains a lack of recognition or respect for the Internet's ability to connect us directly with audiences, bypassing the media completely. In particular, the senior leaders of many agencies simply have not kept up to date, according to industry watchers.

"Senior PR people who aren't tech savvy and would rather read the *New Yorker* will, at a certain point, have to add blogs to their daily news diet," *Newsweek* technology editor and blogger N'Gai Croal told me. "You can't have just your younger entry-level staff being the ones who understand new media."

It's beyond time to wake up because the tools of online media have been in use for several years already, and many of today's practitioners of Internet communications are considerably ahead of the rank–and-file members of the PR profession when it comes to savvy ideas.

Consider, for example, that the definitive *Handbook for Bloggers*, written by Julien Pain and Dan Gillmor, has been online and available *for free* — through the Web site of Paris-based Reporters Without Borders[3] — for several years. Reading it might have prevented PR tech-rush fiascos, like the fake (or "flack") blog "WalmartingAcrossAmerica. com," which was a publicity stunt by Walmart with its PR agency, Edelman Worldwide, to present a more mainstream America face for the retail giant.

The blog, written by a couple named Jim and Laura, featured stories as they drove across America in a recreational vehicle, stopping each night at a different Walmart parking lot. The stories were always favorable to Walmart. The issue was one of honesty and transparency — Walmart paid Jim and Laura. But neither Walmart nor Edelman disclosed that key fact.

Incidentally, "WalmartingAcrossAmerica" actually did not generate significant audience traffic or attention until exposed by *BusinessWeek* for its subterfuge and dishonesty.

---

[3] www.rsf.org

Entire sections of the online environment — particular blogging and social media — are wide-open spaces, with no rules, no boundaries, no best practices, no oversight and little, if any, ethical grounding.

Between all the chaos, change and new forms of media bubbling up, mainstream media and bloggers have gotten increasingly careless — some call it "lazy" — about verifying facts and sources, effectively opening the door to questionable, non-transparent or false information.

Stealth marketing and promotional agencies — representing everyone from motion picture companies, retailers and pharmaceutical manufacturers to political parties and special interest groups — operate, sometimes under false names and false pretenses, in every corner of today's online conversation. It's not unlike the forty-year-old man who joins a teen chat room, pretending to be one of them, except that the goal of stealth agencies is to alter the way we think.

From countless blogs to Facebook,[4] Twitter[5] and a dizzying number of other social media gathering places, people are working behind the scenes to influence and manipulate our perceptions. It's uncharted territory on the Internet and, while widespread, it is the opposite of open, transparent and truthful. Stealth or out in the open, marketing people and some in public relations are online and in hot pursuit of audiences. Specialists and consultants, rather than public relations agencies, are exploring online opportunities and charting new courses.

"Why put out a press release when the content is not newsworthy? Because this is the way they've always done it? Nonsense," I was told by veteran Ottawa, Canada, media and communications consultant Kathryn Schwab,[6] who works in the open, with transparency and integrity, on behalf of her clients. She says:

> *Better to engage in a direct conversation, using the right communications tools, directed at the target audience. If the audience is amassing on Facebook, then get going! If the audience is sitting on a forum, then get on the forum! Yes, it takes work to find the audience, but go find them. Magazines, newspapers and TV are losing audience in*

---

[4] www.facebook.com

[5] www.twitter.com

[6] www.prceptive.com

record numbers each month! Where are they? They are somewhere!

Whatever your level of comfort and skill may be with the online world, the Internet remains fairly new to many public relations agencies. Few agencies are active in blogging or any of today's online conversations. When agencies have gotten involved in online projects, they frequently lost control by needing to hire outside help, and it has not always gone well for clients.

The CEO of one well-known, large public relations agency, for example, told me during a public relations conference that she could still barely figure out how to use e-mail, and she thought that surfing the Web was a time-consuming bother. When I wrote the story on my blog — DavidHenderson.com[7] — the manager of her agency's fairly new Internet group took exception.

He wrote in my blog's online comment section that his agency had "almost 90 people worldwide, about half of which came from social media and longer [term] digital backgrounds." I did some checking and found that compared with the agency's total number of employees, his department represented a mere 7 percent commitment to the online world of communications.

I made a few telephone calls to other public relations agencies and found that, on average, a slight 3 to 8 percent of big agency staffs have been assigned to advising clients about the Internet, blogs, social media and the rest of the fast-moving online environment. Few have valid and meaningful credentials in blogging, social media and the tidal wave shift from mainstream traditional to online media.

Don Bates, a colleague of mine, is founding director of the master's degree program in strategic public relations at George Washington University in Washington, D.C. He has been monitoring trends in new styles of communications for years, so I turned to him for a reality check of where the public relations industry is headed. He said:

> *Most serious agencies are struggling with the question of what's the best model for doing business in the years immediately ahead. But most serious agencies are challenged by a lack of investment capital and the*

---

[7] www.davidhenderson.com

appropriately trained people to make many of the changes that will be required.

They need capital for buying the most up-to-date software and equipment for staying ahead of the continuing boom in video-driven communications. They need capital for hiring and compensating the best people.

They will also have to be conversant, if not expert, in the design, delivery and evaluation of new communications technologies that will go well beyond Facebook, Twitter, LinkedIn and all the others, in the near future.

Big PR, especially, is not moving forward fast enough, certainly has not invested in learning and remains too locked in with the old ways of generating billable hours and "making numbers." And each day, the dynamic world of online media speeds farther and farther from their grasp of true comprehension.

Strategic communications in today's fiercely competitive world mandates clever positioning, understanding audience needs and knowing how to craft timely and meaningful messages that excite people and create results.

"I have been amazed sometimes," Gary Shapiro told me, "by the inability of a CEO not only to deal with the media but to articulate a sentence."

Shapiro is president and chief executive of the powerful and high-profile Consumer Electronics Association (CEA),[8] which has more than 2,100 member companies.

In the vast world of trade associations, CEA's Shapiro is recognized as a dynamic and visionary communicator who knows how to capitalize on media opportunities. One of his primary responsibilities is to speak on behalf of the enormous and diverse industry he represents, and he has earned a good reputation in an industry where the brand of a company is largely formed by media coverage, which is greatly influenced by the charisma, passion and communications skills of the person at the helm.

---

[8] www.ce.org

Each year, the Consumer Electronics Association stages the largest trade show of its type in the world — the Consumer Electronics Show, or CES — which is attended by about 140,000 people who want an early peek at the newest, latest and coolest products and gadgets in the electronics industry. The Consumer Electronics Show is also the biggest annual press event in the world.

For corporate leaders, an opportunity to speak at CES is highly coveted. Chief executive officers and their lieutenants often lobby Shapiro's office for months for a slot in the program. One of Shapiro's responsibilities is to evaluate how well a CEO communicates, in order to get a coveted opportunity to speak at CES.

Yet, surprisingly, in today's highly competitive world, a world in which good communications skills are necessary for leadership, not all chief executives have the ability to articulate a vision for their company or to deliver a clear, lucid message, whether to a large audience during a speech or to one reporter during an interview. In fact, quite a few cannot, and it reflects badly on their organizations.

"How do you come to be a CEO of a major company when you cannot speak publicly?" Shapiro exclaimed, as we met in his office in Arlington, Virginia. "I have wondered how a board makes a decision like that [to hire such a person]."

From a purely practical perspective, a great speaker at CES not only captures invaluable media coverage for his or her own company, but the value of the trade show itself is enhanced.

Several corporate leaders, including Robert Iger of Disney, have used speaking opportunities at CES to recalibrate corporate vision, shake off old perceptions and competitively reposition the images of their organizations. Stock prices often jump because of their visibility, direction and confidence.

When a leader articulates the corporate vision behind a new product, initiative or service and receives glowing reviews by respected journalists, the whole company benefits from sales, customer satisfaction, brand awareness and enhanced shareholder value.

The value of media coverage that reaches vast audiences today has in many cases become exponentially greater and even more credible than advertising, and at a fraction of the cost of paid ads. The credibility of authentic messages in plain language wins out over the predictable and tired clichés of advertising.

On the broader canvas of issues that impact lives of people around the globe, understanding today's melding of traditional and online media with technology has never been more important. The entire newspaper industry, for example, has struggled to stay in business by finding a new and more viable business model online.

In the world of human rights, personal and religious freedoms and equality, an integrated approach to strategic communications planning — including the use of online and traditional media coverage, social media and a responsibly written blog — can make the difference, sometimes even between life and death.

Yet not-for-profit organizations, corporations and government agencies frequently struggle to find ways to get the media's attention and get their stories shared with the proper audiences. They often lack experienced staff to advise on communications strategies and the expertise to reach out at the best time, with the best story angle and message, to engage the right contacts in the media, those who can make a difference.

Mastering the art of great media coverage starts with the person at the top owning a big piece of the responsibility for learning, understanding and practicing the methods for how to make it happen. It requires a meaningful investment of time and hard work that cannot be delegated. But the rewards of enhanced leadership charisma, a highly motivated team and a more exciting vision and image for the organization make it worthwhile.

Top executives must create timely, sharp and relevant stories that appeal to the media, as well as stakeholders, buyers and others; they must also employ unique techniques to get messages to the right people in the media and to create favorable awareness for their organizations or themselves.

The timely and relevant part is particularly important because if what you and your organization have to say is out of sync with today's conversation, no one will pay attention, not matter how hard you try.

As I mentioned early, audiences do not care to hear an organization talk about itself. People only want to know how an organization's products or services benefit them and bring value to their lives. It's a sometimes-harsh reality to accept.

We live in a fiercely competitive world, in which many people clamber to get attention before the mainstream news media that is but a mere skeleton of what it once was, having been financially damaged and mortally wounded by the digital revolution and new media upstarts.

We live in a world where even venerable institutions, like the *New York Times*, compete for audience and revenue with the latest evolving online phenomena like Twitter,[9] Google,[10] YouTube[11] and Politico.[12]

Invest time online for first-hand learning to understand how the online playing field has been leveled; determine what may have merit to meet your objectives and what does not.

Should the head of your organization have a blog and, for that matter, Facebook and Twitter accounts? How can new online technology work to enhance visibility for your organization and provide a more compelling and active image online?

All cool bells and whistles of technology aside, the secrets to accurately communicating news and generating great media attention in this new world order for reaching audiences may sound a little old-fashioned, but they are astonishingly effective:

- Take responsibility as a leader, manager or communicator for being the face and voice of your organization.

- Create visionary messages that people will find captivating.

- Communicate your messages through a clever story. A good story is precisely what the media wants.

- Get to the point quickly and clearly, using words we all understand.

- Interweave your messages throughout all levels of your organization, like a beacon shining on a path to enhance understanding.

- Be consistent, timely, truthful and relevant in your messages.

---

[9] www.twitter.com
[10] www.google.com
[11] www.youtube.com
[12] www.politico.com

- Avoid talking about your organization, instead talking about the value of what your organization does.

These points do not really look like great secrets, after all, do they? It is just practical common sense that reflects how today's style of discourse happens in the digital environment. These techniques effectively capture visibility, regardless of the audience.

The odd part is that most companies and organizations remain mired in worn-out, threadbare tactics and dysfunctional internal politics that hinder the growth of a company's image, reputation and brand. It's time for a refreshing change.

Chapter Four:
Creating Symbolic Images

Perhaps no person has left a greater and more positive imprint on the practice of PR and strategic communications worldwide over the last couple of decades than the late Michael Deaver.

Mike Deaver was sometimes accused of being an expert at media manipulation. It is my guess that whoever alleged that harbored a good deal of envy for his talent. There is no question that Deaver made the contemporary concept of "photo op" into an art form to achieve the rewards of great media coverage, whether "spontaneously" manipulated or otherwise.

Deaver became famous as the image-maker for President Ronald Reagan. He was a master at staging visually memorable symbolic events, from the fall of the Berlin Wall to the fortieth anniversary commemoration of the invasion at Omaha Beach. Deaver's artistry created lasting impressions on millions of us around the world.

Former first lady and friend Nancy Reagan said Deaver's greatest skill was in "arranging what were known as good visuals, televised events or scenes that would leave a powerful symbolic image in people's minds."

Deaver was nearly always behind the scenes, advising not only President Reagan but countless other leaders — heads of state to titans of industry — on the value of speaking with a clear voice and wise perspective. He was a leading example of people who have changed the world by knowing how to communicate a message, inspire greatness and create a lasting great impression.

His secret for great communications was to help a leader develop an ability to translate the most complex issue into just a couple of clear sentences, using simple words that would lead to positive change. In other words, leaders should take a moment to step back from all the chaos, look at the big picture of what needs to be done and say it ... in a few easily understood words.

After leaving the White House, Deaver took his quiet manner and enormous talent to independent PR agency Edelman Worldwide, where he reshaped the practice of public relations and helped successful organizations around the world become even more successful. There, I learned from him and treasured his friendship.

Just before his passing in August 2007, Deaver's colleagues at Edelman asked him to describe the few great communicators he had known, including President Reagan and Dan Edelman, founder of Edelman Worldwide. This is what Deaver said:

"They, and a few of us, got into the world of communications when it was a world of print ... then radio and TV and now the Internet, e-mails and blogs ... and yet their values remain the same today:

- Know who you are.

- Be open and transparent.

- Be ready for change.

"But the world *is changing*," Deaver told his colleagues and friends. He quoted an excerpt from a column by Thomas Friedman in the *New York Times*. Friedman had written:

"When everyone has a blog, a MySpace page or a Facebook entry, everyone is a publisher. When everyone has a cell phone with a camera in it, everyone is a paparazzo. When everyone can upload a video on YouTube, everyone is a filmmaker. We're all public figures now. The blogosphere has made the global discussion so much richer — and each of us so much more transparent. In this transparent world, 'how' you live your life and 'how' you conduct your business matters more than ever because so many people can now see into what you do and tell so many other people about it on their own[,] without any editor."

What was important to Deaver was *how* we differentiate ourselves in a world that has become so exposed and so easily copied. He talked of getting your hows right — how you build trust, how you collaborate, how you lead and how you say you're sorry.

"More people than ever will know about it when you do or don't," he said.

Chapter Five:
Take Charge of Your Own Success

Welcome to life in a fast-paced world, an environment that is constantly changing, taking new shape and then reinventing itself all over again. It is a world in which, for journalists and bloggers, every minute can be a deadline. It is a world in which what you say in Chicago can be reported almost instantly in London, Singapore and everywhere in between via new technologies on the Internet, news services, online social media, streaming video, blogs and satellite television news.

We are living in a world of such exposure, openness and transparency that it almost seems we live on microscopes slides. There is no such thing as secrets anymore.

This is a world in which the diverse and ever-changing dynamics of new information about current events from countless sources compete for the media's attention. It's a world where a faceless blogger can learn or concoct something hostile about your organization, post it on the Web and ruin your whole day.

We are in a world in which the media you knew last year isn't the same media you need to know today, and it most likely will evolve into something different and even more challenging next year.

In today's highly competitive world, media attention — mainstream or online — positions you as a leader, as someone with a valued voice. Having the media write about your organization builds *your* reputation and enhances *your* brand. It builds word-of-mouth awareness.

Yet for many individuals, businesses and organizations that aim to reach wide audiences, effective strategic communications remains all too elusive, as many prefer, instead, to use tactic after tactic in a vain struggle to find something that works. Lacking an overarching strategy, tactics will always fail.

Corporations spend millions on public relations efforts, trying to win favorable positioning in their respective marketplaces by using the awesome reach of the media, which is still a powerful conduit to the public. Yet objectives are not met, and many organizations feel shortchanged.

Often lacking the expertise in-house, even within their own corporate communications departments, organizations hire public relations agencies in an attempt to achieve prominent media coverage. However, many agencies themselves lack meaningful skills, contacts and know-how. It is no secret that PR agencies no longer, as a general rule, invest in adequate staff training to build competence at strategic communications, writing or other client service skills.

Why? To find the answer, one must look behind the veil of ownership of many agencies today. Public relations agencies used to be independently owned, and many reflected a distinctive regional or national savvy level of expertise. Clients benefited from the competitiveness, internal pride and cross-discipline teamwork that came from independence. That's no longer always the case for many agencies, especially the larger or specialized ones.

Massive financially driven, publicly traded advertising conglomerates have been gobbling up formerly independent public relations, advertising and marketing firms, including most major agencies, during much of the last decade.

Omnicom Group now owns Fleishman-Hillard, Porter Novelli, Cone, and Ketchum, to name just a few of its hundreds of holdings. WPP owns Burson-Marsteller, Hill and Knowlton, GCI Group, and Ogilvy among its galaxy of PR and advertising firms. French giant Publicis Groupe owns Manning Selvage & Lee Public Relations, headquartered in New York. And the list goes on.

These enormous multinational conglomerates, many based in Europe, own hundreds of public relations, marketing, public affairs, branding and advertising agencies, and consultancies. The holding companies view agencies and consultancies as moneymaking machines, and they demand big payoffs. In this world of conglomerates, high billable hours and tight-fisted control of budgets equal ever-increasing profits. It's solely about money.

Incidentally, you may seek a public relations agency and consider four agencies that are all owned by the same multinational advertising holding company, only to have a couple drop out for conflict-of-interest reasons because they represent your competitors. However, when you select another agency, the ultimate beneficiary of profits from your account may be the same holding company that owns the agencies that originally dropped out of the bidding.

The agency holding company concept is rewarding sometimes for investors but causes an obsession on extracting as much money from clients as possible while keeping overhead low. For agency managers, it is often an untenable situation — make your numbers or else. The "or else" part means the manager may not get a bonus or promotion or, in the worst case, may lose his or her job completely. Needless to say, staff training has taken a backseat to making the financial numbers.

In an environment in which employees are expected to bill at least seven and a half hours each workday to client work, internal training programs at even the largest PR agencies are woefully lacking or do not exist; professional education to build or improve skills pulls agency personnel away from client billable hours.

The emphasis on billable time is similar to that of law firms. However, the big difference is that lawyers graduate from law schools better trained and prepared when they are initially hired than are most young graduates who join PR shops without any practical experience.

Within the public relations industry, agency veterans are beginning to criticize the lack of training as being incredibly shortsighted, and thus leading to the possibility of shallow work for clients.

Doug Poretz, of the independently owned Qorvis Communications[13] in Washington, believes the fundamental model of most public relations agencies is "broken and outmoded." Poretz maintains that the only thing today's clients want are value and results, yet most agencies sell time, what he calls "an outdated commodity."

There is a clear and obvious disconnect, according to Poretz. PR service providers are selling something the customers don't want. He also maintains that the hourly billing model is to blame for high employee and client turnover at many public relations agencies.

---

[13] www.qorvis.com

Qorvis, a relatively new agency, has grown rapidly on the PR scene, partly because it snagged a multimillion dollar account: the attempt to polish the image of Saudi Arabia in the wake of the September 11, 2001, terrorist attacks.

Qorvis' business model is likely to succeed; the future of its client relationships is based on performance and measurable results rather than billable hours.

Mike Figliuolo shares the opinion that agency model of traditional public relations is broken. He is managing director of Thought Leaders, LLC[14] — a national leadership development training firm. He says:

> I've seen many PR people clinging to the old business model of fee for service versus fees based on impact. Any compensation model based on hourly rates is fundamentally flawed in many cases as it creates an incentive for the firm to work slower and generate less valuable work for their clients.

"On the other hand, a model where an agency is rewarded for impact aligns client and agency incentives, and creates a push within the agency to be as efficient and effective as possible," Figliuolo shared with me from his office in Columbus, Ohio.

"Some of that efficiency and effectiveness comes in the form of using new tools that have become ubiquitous (blogging, social media, better Web sites, online communities, etc.). Given the antiquated business models at many agencies, there's no imperative for them to embrace these new tools. Therefore, they're riding a dying trend," he said.

The head of corporate communications for a leading Fortune 500 corporation, who asked to remain anonymous, agrees that today's PR agency model is broken and obsolete.

"Too often," he said, "they want to counsel and strategize rather than be accountable for action and results."

He went on to explain that many of the top PR agencies use a standard format to handle a client's brand, reputation or media challenge. Regardless of the industry or uniqueness of the client or situation, the agencies use cookie cutter approaches with little or no customization.

---

[14] www.thoughtleadersllc.com

The fate of even a multibillion dollar organization's brand and public reputation is often placed in the hands of junior level, lower-paid and sometimes ill-prepared PR agency staff. These inexperienced staff members are charged with figuring out how to communicate your news and gain publicity without messing things up. Guess who is blamed and canned first when PR programs crash and burn?

You may wonder whether public relations agencies really care to accomplish good results on your behalf and at your expense. The answer is often yes. But far too many agencies — especially the big, multinational firms owned by publicly traded holding companies — care more about getting their hands on your fat budget than helping your reputation or getting solid results.

To ensure that a PR agency is focused on results, my unnamed acquaintance at a Fortune 500 corporation suggests that you ask your PR agency these overly candid questions and measure their responses:

- What skill set do you value most in your people? Writing skills, humility and outside agency experience are all good and extremely rare answers.

- How do you incentivize your people through base and variable compensation? Run away, he said, if growth is mentioned before customer satisfaction.

- What metrics do you use to measure customer satisfaction? Look for a clear answer that indicates, for example, customer surveys or increased favorable press. If the agency people awkwardly measure their words or look at each other in search of an answer, walk away.

- Will you contract on a pay-for-performance basis? The best agencies will at least consider this option, as it ties their performance to your organization. Watch their expressions when you ask this question.

These are challenging yet fair questions. Within today's context of the big agency model, such questions are completely appropriate. Agency margins are under pressure from holding companies, and when agencies hire and fire staff as they win and lose clients, they find it difficult to attract and keep the best talent. You want to be sure that skilled employees are attracted to and maintained on your account.

Some of the most-recognized names in the public relations industry have self-serving business models that focus on making money to keep the holding company beast happy. Such agencies are experts more at getting your business rather than keeping it.

PR insiders call the practice "churn and burn." Agency leaders generate as much new business as possible and then immediately hand it off to lower-paid staff, who are billed out at embarrassingly high rates despite their junior level of expertise. The agency assumes that clients will hang with them for at least a year; a grace period allows for mistakes. By the time a client finally fires the agency for poor performance, agency leaders have moved on and snagged newer clients.

Chapter Six:
Road Map of the New Online World

The online world is a trendy place, known for the latest clever, new idea or popular site to check out. With funny names like Twitter, Yelp,[15] Present.ly,[16] Yammer,[17] Blip.fm[18] and JackBe,[19] how does anyone make sense of it? The only practical answer, I am afraid, is to get online and take the time to explore what works best for your communication objectives.

It's an upside-down world of communications. How can executives and communications professionals transition from traditional styles to the new online environment in order to attract attention and communicate accurately, effectively and transparently? How do they get a handle on the new world of social media, blogs, Twitter and Facebook?

A good place to start is becoming grounded in some of the new terminology:

- Web 2.0 — Widely regarded as the second generation of Internet styles and designed, known for information sharing, collaboration and interactivity.

- Blog — The definition of blog has evolved into different kinds of interactive and information-sharing Web sites, ranging from individual blogs with regular entries of commentary, images

---

[15] www.yelp.com
[16] www.presentlyapp.com
[17] www.yammer.com
[18] http://blip.fm
[19] www.jackbe.com

- and video, to more sophisticated blogs for corporations and the news media. The Web sites of MSNBC, *People* magazine, *China Journal*, *Wall Street Journal Law*, Boston College Center for Corporate Citizenship, and Network Solutions are just a few examples of large organizations using blog technology for online visibility.

- Social media — Quite simply, it's sharing information online. "A shift in how people discover, read and share news, information and content. It's a fusion of sociology and technology, transforming monologue (one to many) into dialogue (many to many), and is the democratization of information, transforming people from content readers into publishers. Social media has become extremely popular because it allows people to connect in the online world to form relationships for personal and business," according to the online collaborative encyclopedia project Wikipedia.[20]

The category of online social media has exploded in popularity, and examples are all over the place. Businesspeople create profiles, build networks of contacts and share tips on the social media site LinkedIn.[21] Twitter, Facebook, Yelp and Flickr[22] are different kinds of social media.

Twitter — a free, mini-blogging service — bills itself as "a service for friends, family and co-workers to communicate and stay connected through the exchange of quick, frequent" sharing of information. Users are limited to 140 characters in what they can post.

In discussing Twitter with a veteran journalist at Radio Free Europe in Prague, he observed that it appeared similar to the cryptic style of telegraph dispatches in days gone by. He quickly told me with a wink that he had only read about such dispatches in history books, and that he had no firsthand knowledge.

Facebook was originally created for college students to connect, and it has expanded to anyone. Facebook's users, who number in the millions, can create profiles, upload photos and build online communities

---

[20] www.wikipedia.org
[21] www.linkedin.com
[22] www.flickr.com

of friends around the world with whom to share information. One of the distinctive features of Facebook is the ability to find lost relatives and friends and reestablish contact.

Yelp helps people find good local businesses, lodging and restaurants through the comments and opinions of user reviews. For example, my wife and I used Yelp to check out recommendations on hotels in California as we planned a vacation there. More than 20 million people visit Yelp's Web site each month.

Flickr is an online community for anyone to manage images and share personal photos with others. The Vancouver, British Columbia, company claims that more than three billion images have been uploaded to Flickr since the site was launched in 2004.

These are just a few of the dozens of online social media services for sharing information in nearly any language. Some, such as Twitter, have become important online communications methods for public relations professionals to use. Twitter, for example, is actively monitored by most major news organizations and has become a new way for communications professional to present story ideas to specific people in the media.

Perhaps the best way to better connect with all of an organization's publics, including the media, is to use a more contemporary approach for an online newsroom. In the past, a company's online newsroom, often inaccurately labeled a "pressroom," has typically been little more than a lifeless, dull press release depository. As such, it's of little value to reporters or other visitors looking for news updates and information.

The usual style of an online newsroom has often presented a challenge for any journalist who needs to find even basic information quickly, such as an appropriate media contact. The online newsroom of Ford,[23] for example, requires a journalist to fill out an online form and then wait for a response. While it may be convenient for Ford's PR people, such a procedure might cause a delay for a reporter on deadline.

It seems obvious that any smart company now has to position its expertise and experience prominently online in order to achieve the following:

---

[23] www.ford.com/about-ford/news-announcements

- Be clearly heard and stand out in all the right ways.
- Manage the conversation around its image and reputation.
- Be timely and relevant.

The hard part is expressing its corporate voice above the noise of the marketplace, where often people much less qualified — but far more vocal — pump out their opinions into mainstream and online social media. The sheer speed, volume and rapid dissemination of information — right or wrong — can inundate communications and sway public opinion.

A company's "Googleability," and the news that appears about it on page one of any search engine, often can determine its believability.

To have a meaningful conversation online, a company needs to do the following:

- Articulate clear points of view on the things that it cares about the most.

- Identify its own experts and champions to tell compelling stories to advance its case and strengthen its market position.

- Create ever-evolving public platforms and forums where it can consistently and frequently showcase its views, along with other respected industry experts and thought leaders.

- Create a forum for sharing comments, generating a conversation and listening.

For example, the team at The News Group Net LLC,[24] of which I am a partner, developed a groundbreaking online newsroom for the Imperial Sugar Company (ISC) that has focused on delivering legitimate and timely news about the company and the global sugar industry. A primary objective of the landmark ISC Newsroom[25] has been to credibly present a more balanced and accurate point of view about the company than is reported in the more sensationally oriented mainstream media.

---

[24] www.thenewsgroup.net
[25] www.iscnewsroom.com

When an explosion and resulting fires temporarily closed Imperial Sugar Company's large sugar refinery at Port Wentworth, Ga., in February 2008, many news stories and images of the incident appeared in mainstream and online media, including at Google and other search engines. Those reports about fire, death and tragedy continued to show up on the first pages of search engines for months even though much of the information became outdated.

The online newsroom has delivered the latest news about Imperial Sugar Company rebuilding its refinery, resumption of sugar production, business expansion and other relevant stories about business and community involvement that the mainstream media considers to be less dramatic. The newsroom has assisted in positioning Imperial Sugar Company as an authoritative voice in the sugar industry before numerous important audiences, including shareholders, employees, government agencies, customers, business partners and industry analysts, as well as the media.

Quite simply, Imperial Sugar Company's landmark online newsroom has served as a one-stop shop for the best thinking and views on the company and the sugar industry along with the surrounding issues and market forces.

In this digital era, timeliness and relevance are crucial. Online is an environment of conversations, sharing, interaction, responsiveness and engagement. It's all needed in order to achieve meaningful and sustained communications. An organization's online newsroom must reflect a business that is open, transparent and interested in accurate and timely communications.

Another good example is Samsung's newsroom.[26] The giant consumer electronics company is using the dynamic, popular and interactive blog technology for its online newsroom. All the latest news, media contacts and events are clearly presented, enabling the media to quickly find what they need.

An online newsroom no longer needs to be a dusty and boring archive of news materials that go back for years. Rather, it can become an online showcase for an organization's latest news, resources, information, background, photos, audio and video, and a place to listen, exchange ideas and share with key audiences.

---

[26] www.samsungusanews.com

An objective of a new-style online newsroom is to make it appeal to all audiences with a fresh and appealing flow of updates and interactive features.

On the other hand, traditional Web sites, using old-style HTML coding — the kind of sites most businesses and organizations still have — often appear static, lifeless and about as boring as a dog-eared business card. Such sites may have an animated element, using technology called flash, but even that style started going out of fashion around 2006. Additionally, and this is an important factor, HTML sites are just not particularly search engine friendly. Prominent search engine ranking equates to improved awareness.

Today's most popular and appealing sites are driven by a completely different online engine — utilizing software originally intended for blogs — and have a spectrum of dynamic tools for viewing pictures and playing video and audio. They have interactive features, giving visitors the freedom to e-mail stories, post comments or share information on social media sites.

These sites will provide visitors the opportunity to subscribe and receive all updates by e-mail whenever news and updates happen, instantly and automatically.

One trend is toward the use of Wordpress[27] software. Wordpress functions like the engine "under the hood," powering tens of millions of interactive online sites, ranging from the *New York Times*, *Le Monde*, Anderson Cooper 360 and Boston College to the personal blog of Sir Richard Branson, many corporate newsrooms and Larry King's CNN blog. Wordpress software has become the contemporary online standard, and the best part is … it's free.

Themes for Wordpress or design templates give each blog or site a unique look, and it can be customized, reflecting the image branding and feel of any business, organization or personality. The best themes for Wordpress are not free, but they are reasonably priced.

The meteoric popularity of Wordpress has created a sizable cottage industry of theme designers, in addition to hundreds of software developers who create what are called plug-ins or feature-packed add-on elements for Wordpress.

---

[27] www.wordpress.org

Wordpress and similar technologies will make sites more search engine friendly, an incredibly important factor in today's online environment. Any organization needs all the help possible to increase a footprint of awareness online.

The best part is that when news updates are posted on a blog-powered online newsroom, they will show up on Google, Yahoo and other search engines within minutes.

The technique is called search engine optimization, or SEO, and building sites on blog technology provides a multitude of tools, plug-ins and methods for boosting a site's ranking among search engines.

You can see where I am going with this. In today's digital environment, an organization must embrace new ideas and try something different and bold. It must stop promoting itself and stop shouting because no one is listening or cares amid all the competitive clutter. We must join the discussion online, where the audiences are.

There's a new opportunity today to reach out to the media, investors, stakeholders, customers and others who are important to your organization, engaging them online through rich information resources. It's neither difficult nor costly, in most cases.

The new style of online newsrooms will help focus audience attention back to an organization and back to more managed information and messages. It will contribute to being viewed and perceived as a trusted and reliable information resource.

We have all this affordable and highly effective new technology readily at hand today. Using it effectively just might lead to a competitive advantage.

Chapter Seven:
Twitter Dispatches in 140 Characters

When Twitter burst onto the online world, no one knew what to do with it. Here was a free mini-blogging service built around the idea of posting short 140-character instant online updates. The concept was to find people to follow while creating a group of followers and, all the while, posting mini-dispatches online.

Many professionals find Twitter to be an invaluable online tool, providing access to networks of people who might otherwise be out of reach.

Looking closely at how Twitter is being used, especially by businesspeople, many are defining boundaries as an efficient way to minimize time on the service — such as to capture and share news and events they find of interest; as a listening tool to learn about new concepts and what others are talking about; to announce news and engage with outside resources; or to drive visitor traffic to a blog.

Twitter at first became popular as the latest online fad, and it was dismissed, even demeaned, by the mainstream media. Then, Mumbai happened.

In November 2008, there were an estimated ten coordinated terrorist attacks and bombings across the port city of Mumbai, India's financial capital and largest metropolitan area. The attacks lasted three days, killing at least 173 people. A Pakistan-based militant group was blamed.

The world watched live pictures of burning hotels and people running for cover. Inside the hotels and buildings under siege, innocent people were trapped by the violence and fires. They hid, not knowing whether the person on the other side of a door might be a terrorist or not. Many used iPhones and Blackberry wireless devices to send e-mails and text messages to loved ones and friends around the world. Many also posted continuous updates on events on Twitter. It was real-time citizen journalism — live from the scene — and the whole world woke up and paid attention to the power and value of Twitter.

In June 2009, Twitter, Facebook, YouTube and other online social media channels made history by eclipsing the world's mainstream news media as leading forms of mass communication in the aftermath of the controversial and disputed presidential election in Iran. Even though the country's theocratic rulers attempted to stifle press coverage, political revolution was coordinated in part through 140-character Twitter dispatches that were read and shared instantly around the world.

At one point in the crisis, the United States State Department asked executives of Twitter to postpone scheduled maintenance of its Internet servers in order not to interrupt the flow of news and information. Twitter had become a vital global link to a nation in turmoil. Twitter citizen journalist groups identified by characteristic hash marks (#) were carrying hundreds of messages a second, such as #IranElection, #Neda and #Iran. It was an avalanche of personal eyewitness reports, rumors and updates.

Twitter has quickly evolved into one of the digital era's most important sources for information and news. The service attracts millions of new members, giving rise to a new protocol for sharing information in the Internet age. Even the mainstream media has become an active participant, inviting people to submit story ideas through Twitter.

The unofficial Twitter protocol is similar to other social media sites: Be nice to other people, be open and sharing, be informative and strive to be accurate.

Twitter has given rise to entirely new communities of shared interests online. If, for example, you are interested in music or growing flowers or networking among business colleagues, Twitter provides a platform for anyone to develop a personal group of followers and people to follow. Even Oprah and actress Tina Fey have joined Twitter.

Yet the social media phenomenon of Twitter is not for everyone. David Martin, vice president of primary research at Neilson Online, wrote on the Nielsen Wire blog[28] that more than 60 percent of U.S. Twitter users fail to return the following month. In other words, Twitter's audience retention rate, or the percentage of a given month's users who come back the following month, is about 40 percent.

The Twitter quitters, Martin wrote, are a roadblock to Twitter's long-term growth as an influential forum online.

Twitter has also not been without its share of social media controversies. In one flap that gained attention worldwide, a PR agency account executive named James Andrews posted the following on Twitter as he arrived in Memphis, Tenn., creating one of the first examples of an online social media crisis:

> *True confession but I'm in one of those towns where I scratch my head and say, "I would die if I had to live here."*

The fellow had flown to Memphis to visit FedEx, one of the largest clients of his employer, Ketchum Public Relations, reportedly to talk with the corporate communications people at FedEx about how to use online social media.

Someone who worked for FedEx was following Andrews on Twitter, and that person shared the post among the top executives at the FedEx front office, as well as the company's corporate communications staff. At that point, a person in the FedEx corporate communications staff apparently took umbrage to the post and responded with this personal e-mail message:

> *Mr. Andrews, [if] I interpret your post correctly, these are your comments about Memphis a few hours after arriving in the global headquarters city of one of your key and lucrative clients, and the home of arguably one of the most important entrepreneurs in the history of business, FedEx founder Fred Smith. Many of my peers and I feel this is inappropriate. We do not know the total millions of dollars FedEx Corporation pays Ketchum annually for the valuable and important work your company does for us around the globe. We are confident, however, it is*

---

[28] http://blog.nielsen.com/nielsenwire

enough to expect a greater level of respect and awareness from someone in your position as a vice president at a major global player in your industry. A hazard of social networking is [that] people will read what you write.

Not knowing exactly what prompted your comments, I will admit the area around our airport is a bit of an eyesore, not without crime, prostitution, commercial decay and a few potholes. But there is a major political, community, religious and business effort underway, [which] includes FedEx, to transform that area. We're hopeful that over time, our city will have a better "face" to present to visitors.

James, everyone participating in today's event, including those in the auditorium with you this morning, just received their first paycheck of 2009, containing a 5 percent pay cut … which we wholeheartedly support because it continued the tradition established by Mr. Smith of doing whatever it takes to protect jobs. Considering that we just entered the second year of a U.S. recession, and we are experiencing significant business loss due to the global economic downturn, many of my peers and I question the expense of paying Ketchum to produce the video open for today's event, work that could have been achieved by internal award-winning professionals with decades of experience in television production.

Additionally, Mr. Andrews, with all due respect, to continue the context of your post, true confession: Many of my peers and I don't see much relevance between your presentation this morning and the work we do in Employee Communications.

(Signed as a personal message by a member of the FedEx Corporate Communications team.)

No one knows how it happened, but the e-mail was leaked publicly and shared by many people around the world. The CEO of a major trade association forwarded it to me, and he had learned about it from a person at a major public relations agency other than Ketchum.

In a nanosecond, it had become not only embarrassing for all concerned — but juicy cyber-gossip as well. Popular blogger Peter Shankman posted the e-mail on his blog,[29] attracting thousands of readers. The *Huffington Post*[30] picked it up from Shankman, and awareness spread. But no one bothered to confirm the story. No one — neither Shankman nor Huffington — checked the facts, preferring instead to post and recycle gossip online, and their audiences grew overnight.

Walt Mossberg, the highly respected reporter at the *Wall Street Journal*, told me a couple of years ago that he did not consider many bloggers to be journalists because they lacked the training, disciplines and ethical standards of legitimate newspeople, and here was an example of Mossberg's sage perspective coming true. Bloggers were recycling gossip about the Ketchum-FedEx-Twitter flap without regard for even the most basic ethics of journalism, accuracy or fairness to the parties involved.

Curious about how an unsubstantiated rumor could spin out of control so quickly online and through e-mails, I attempted to get a comment from Andrews and Ray Kotcher, CEO of Ketchum but got no response at first. The corporate communications department at FedEx, however, was immediately open and transparent in confirming the story, names and events. FedEx issued this statement:

> *This is an unfortunate situation and demonstrates very poor judgment by Mr. Andrews. The reaction by our employees proves once again that FedEx takes great pride in our hometown of Memphis. This lapse in judgment also demonstrates the need to apply fundamental communications principles in the evolving social networking environment: Think before you speak; be careful of you what you say and how you say it. Mr. Andrews made a mistake, and he has apologized. We are moving on.*

---

[29] shankman.com
[30] www.huffingtonpost.com

After FedEx issued its statement, Ketchum Public Relations eventually sent me the following e-mail:

> *It was a lapse in judgment, and we've apologized to our client. We greatly value this long-standing client relationship. It is our privilege to work with them.*

By the time both companies had given me these statements, their Twitter crisis had been brewing online for several days. Hundreds of thousands of people were on social media Web sites, discussing, sharing and judging the propriety of what had happened.

What I noted on my blog — DavidHenderson.com — at the time was the seeming lack of awareness about the online social media crisis that was happening. Neither the PR agency nor the shipping company appeared to be aware of what was occurring online. Ketchum and FedEx instead used an old-style PR approach, in my opinion, to point the finger of blame at the junior person. I don't think anyone gets off that easily in today's online world, in which Ketchum appeared to behave, in this example, as a novice.

The scenario this painted is how badly big PR has grasped today's interactive Web 2.0 world of openness, transparency and accuracy. It also demonstrated an astonishing level of hubris and/or lack of knowledge for how the media, Web 2.0 or otherwise works, in my opinion.

In a world that has shifted to a style of communications that emphasizes listening, engaging and sharing, many big PR agencies remain locked in a decades-old habit of creating vast amounts of publicity materials to be pushed at audiences on behalf of clients. It is one-sided style of shouting and might be called propaganda in some places around the world. The approach, however, is obsolete and not the best way to reach today's audiences, online or otherwise.

Whatever it is labeled, the old-fashioned style of PR is the antithesis of communications in today's interactive Web 2.0 world, and it is the opposite of what audiences and the media need. Reporters — legitimate and trained journalists — require stories, perspective, interviews and a chance to write both sides. The same holds true for blogging journalists because blogging is the new media.

Ketchum PR, which had no corporate blog or Twitter presence at the time, relinquished any chance at managing its image in the online discussions.

Referring back to an earlier chapter in this book and what entrepreneur Mark Cuban had shared with me: "Executives have to learn how to shape information about themselves and their companies, or the Internet will do it for them, and it won't be pretty."

We have entered a new era in the United States, where a leader, our new president, has called for principled behavior and an end to the partisanship and nastiness that has so permeated our society. And so, all of us — or at least many of us — are trying to figure out how to mirror that behavior in various aspects of our lives. We have to get away from the nastiness and partisanship.

We all make mistakes. But what the employee of Ketchum Public Relations posted on Twitter about Memphis appeared to be nasty in tone, at least to one person at FedEx. In a world that fundamentally is all about relationships, Andrews allegedly dissed the town, and in doing so, he mocked the decision by his employer's major client, FedEx, to have that city as its home.

Such behavior online suggests, in my view, that Ketchum Public Relations, a company owned by the enormous PR and advertising agency holding company Omnicom Group, apparently did not understand the changing discourse of conversation, the new spirit of change hoped for in America or the online world of new media.

We are living in a time when millions of people are looking for a unific way to communicate, to change our language and to rise above the mean-spirited sniping and partisan jibs that have become an infectious form of our communication.

In the mix of all that has been said, the heart of the matter has to do with trying to change an atmosphere that promotes nastiness, a snide laugh by belittling somebody else. That's the absolute core.

This is the call of the administration of President Barack Obama, and it applies just as much to the government as to our corporate relationships. We find it amusing to arrogantly put somebody down, and that sort of behavior must stop in order for our country to move forward.

Regardless of the communications method — whether Twitter, a blog, television news, radio, newspapers — the underlying principles of working with journalists as well as our clients, customers, colleagues and friends remain the same. Openness. Transparency. Accuracy. Honesty. Relationships. Respect.

The reality of today's digital environment is that a crisis can spin out of control globally in a nanosecond because people all over the world have access in new ways that did not exist before the advent of the Internet and the interactive communications tools of Web 2.0. Our best defense when it comes to managing reputations online is to learn the rules and protocol of the new environment and behave professionally.

Chapter Eight:
Find Something That Works

How can you find a smart communications strategist, specialist and/or a savvy public relations agency that provides valuable assistance, really "gets it" and delivers the results you expect?

After interviewing leaders of companies, associations and not-for-profit organizations, I repeatedly heard four general warning signs that may help you identify ineffective agencies or strategists:

- Too lopsided a budget versus work discussion. If an agency seems more interested in the size of your budget than in your expectations for hiring an agency, beware.

- Too many expensive suits in the room. If an agency has too many senior level people in the room, beware. Let's get real … they show up for window dressing. Don't count on them to do much work on your account.

- Too much talk, too little listening. If agency representatives talk too much about how great their agency is while not listening to your needs, beware.

- Too much arrogance. If an agency seems too full of its ego, beware. Too much ego can suggest too little competence.

It is important to look behind the curtains — the smoke and mirrors — for a reality check about today's public relations industry. What you find may help you decide whether you need an outside agency or more expertise in-house.

In conducting research for this book, I found that the greatest fundamental flaw among public relations agencies is a failure to recognize and respect the power of the Internet as a strategic tool for connecting with audiences, including the media.

Even today, many agencies often fail to deliver, especially in the area of helping clients build meaningful conversations with audiences.

Part of the reason is that few people who are assigned to communicate with publics or deal with the media have the deep experience and skills it takes to achieve results in today's dynamic merging of mainstream media with online opportunities.

Perhaps more troubling is that many agencies have not kept pace with developments in today's digital and online revolution. Even though agencies boast of their knowledge of the blogging, social media and the online world, few have personal, hands-on experience.

I turned to my colleague David Meerman Scott, a best-selling author and thought leader[31] who lectures worldwide about trends and styles in communications, for his perspective on the direction public relations is headed.

"Prior to the Web, organizations had to communicate to their publics using the media as the mouthpiece," Scott told me. "Now we are going through a revolution because organizations can communicate to their publics directly, through Web sites, blogs, YouTube videos and through social networking sites like forums, chat rooms, Twitter and Facebook.

"There is still room for a few specialist media relations agencies. However, the vast majority of PR agencies need to adapt to the revolution, or go bust. Agencies need to be a part of the new forms of communications."

Scott's thoughts are practical and forward-looking, leading to this starter checklist to use when vetting any PR agency, in order to test their tech savviness and strategic thinking. (Note: If any agency hesitates in their answers or if they pause and exchange glances, cross them off.)

- Ask who in agency leadership is active on Twitter, and whether they are engaging in conversations or just promoting/selling the agency. Get on Twitter yourself and check them out.

---

[31] www.davidmeermanscott.com

- Visit an agency's blogs. Are they one-way sales promotions, or are they engaging people in conversations and listening?

- Visit the agency's YouTube, Facebook and Twitter accounts. Are they sharing good information, and are they reaching out to authentically connect?

- As thought leaders, what books or articles have agency leaders written, especially on today's seismic shifts in communications? (This helps to cull the talkers from the doers.)

Notice how most of the questions center around whether agencies themselves are engaging in the digital revolution. Anyone can create a blog today. A blog is no longer unique. You don't need an agency to send out a press release into oblivion through a costly blast e-mail spam service. Just hire an intern.

What is really important is top-level strategic thinking focused on how technology is used to carry forward messages, image and reputation in order to successfully connect with audiences in this new world of communications.

But that is not necessarily the direction or the business model of most agencies today. Rather, it's about money, and how much an agency can bill a client without being accused of larceny.

"I reviewed three PR agency proposals lately, and all seemed — though from very big agencies — archaic," Steve Kayser shared with me. Kayser manages the online reputation of Cincom, a respected business software company headquartered in Cincinnati, Ohio. Kayser is well known in the online world.[32]

"They wanted about $400,000 per year to build a Web presence, strengthen the brand and introduce the company to social media. The first three months were to be spent on 'immersing themselves in our business,' or learning. Thereafter, the agencies said they would start building a Web site and one blog. Yet, their Web site concepts were dated and one-dimensional," Kayser observed.

Prior to making their proposals, the three agencies had failed to discover that Kayser himself is a respected visionary and opinion leader in the blogging and online social media world. He is one of the best.

---

[32] www.writingriffs.com

Yet the agencies apparently were not active online, or had not bothered to find out. Clearly, they hadn't done their homework.

"That *immersing stuff* is good work — if you can get it," Kayser said with a chuckle. Incidentally, he solved his company's online challenge by building the online sites himself at a fraction of the cost.

What Kayser experienced is common: Senior members of an agency, whose primary job is to find new clients, recycled old-school ideas, sometimes amateurishly wrapped in contemporary jargon. For professionals more knowledgeable about the digital revolution, such as Kayser and his company, the proposals from PR agencies do seem to be "archaic."

"PR has become a much more disciplined field, where agency people usually keep track of how they spend each hour of the day," observes Jack O'Dwyer. He should know. O'Dwyer has been reporting on the public relations industry in his O'Dwyer publications for four decades.

"Propelling this discipline is the fact that the great majority of the 15 biggest PR firms have been acquired by the large advertising agency holding (or financial investment) companies. Management and financial controls have become standard in a field once known for its looseness. Worldwide accounts in the multimillion-dollar category demand such controls if PR firms are to keep control of their costs."

Yet issues of quick, big profits and return on investment aside, doesn't this business model reflect old-fashioned thinking at the expense of effective communications in the new online media world? Or does it suggest a scramble for a fast buck?

It's not all gloom and doom in the public relations industry. Independent and smaller agencies are making solid inroads, even when head-to-head with the big guys, by simply delivering better results.

Chaim Haas is an expert in this field, and an example of today's new breed of communications professional. A remarkably well-connected executive at Kaplow Public Relations[33] in New York, he is somewhat of a rarity in his industry. He knows mainstream media, as well as the online world of bloggers, and the importance of reaching out directly to various publics about as well as anyone.

---

[33] www.kaplowpr.com

Despite his extensive knowledge of technology, he doesn't hesitate to use the telephone as an alternative method to connect with an influential blogger, except that Haas uses the services of Skype — the online communications service, and his client — to make his calls.

He knows that a personal connection through a call, rather than e-mail, often leads to a trusted and respected relationship.

Haas likes to paraphrase Yoda, the protagonist in *Star Wars*: "There is no try, only do," he says. He is known as a doer.

"The ways of communication — be they traditional journalists, online journalists, bloggers or direct to consumer — are converging, and we must be able to do each one of these things exceptionally well," Haas told me.

He sees today's style of communications as one big collaborative conversation in which everyone has something to share.

"With a blog, you can have a ripple effect into mainstream media," Haas says. "Bloggers can uncover interesting consumer stories on how technology is used. Reporters follow bloggers for story ideas just as consumers follow bloggers for information. Everyone is actively in the conversation."

As a result, Kaplow has a resident blogger on staff to listen, monitor online buzz and undercover story ideas and blog postings relevant to the agency's clients and that have the potential of being pitched for favorable coverage by mainstream media to benefit clients.

Kaplow's business model is significantly ahead of most public relations agencies. Everyone at the agency has practical usage and know-how about online communications tools. Instead of a smallish, centralized group, the entire staff is educated on how to use the latest methods of the digital revolution, making Kaplow a successful model for the PR agency industry.

Unfortunately, I had a different experience as head of global communications for Gulfstream Aerospace, a worldwide business aircraft corporation. My company was a client of a major international public relations agency, which I inherited when I took the job. I found that although the PR agency had offices in far-flung world capitals, each office was its own profit center and, consequently, each operated in its own insular silo, rarely sharing important information about clients unless absolutely necessary. That style of doing business remains the same today at many big agencies.

Communications among offices was cautious to the point of being secretive for fear of losing business to another office within the same agency. When Gulfstream needed support services from several of the agency's offices, the hourly billing rates were shocking. I had the impression that each regional office viewed our business as manna from heaven.

Here is an example: When we asked for the agency's offices in Los Angeles, London and Hong Kong to help at an event by sending two or three people, nearly everyone in the office showed up, including the top managers, who were billed at more than $400 an hour, and just stood around. We also discovered, much to our aggravation, that the agency's offices did not share information about our events, so we had to brief each office from scratch, which also increased billable hours.

Incidentally, the PR agency seemed to work hardest when attempting to claim credit for our brand- and reputation-building successes, even though their contribution was insignificant at the time.

During many interviews with corporations, organizations and PR agencies — in addition to the media — in preparation to write this book, I found that similar performance by even the largest global public relations agencies is fairly commonplace. They might be huge, employ many people, have multiple offices (which is usually accomplished through the purchase of existing agencies) and make tons of money, but they still operate in silos, and the level of expertise among offices is inconsistent. It's a sadly dismal yet accurate picture.

On the other hand, such an environment presents tremendous opportunities for the C-level executive who wants to learn how to capture the media spotlight and establish a reputation as a compelling and charismatic leader.

Let's expand that earlier checklist of tips to help you find a public relations agency that can deliver top quality results for your organization:

- Size does not matter. The size of a PR agency today is meaningless and not relevant to quality of work. In fact, there is some belief that today's super-sized global agencies have been grown that large only in order to charge super-sized fees. That may work for large clients with significant budgets that get an ego thrill by dropping the name of their agency, but it does not always equate to meaningful results. What's far more important is solid expertise to specifically deliver solutions that will help you become more successful.

- Reputation within your own business arena. Ask your colleagues, customers and even competitors what PR agency they believe delivers the best results.

- Be sure the agency really understands the business you are in. So many client-agency relationships fail because the agency does not fully understand a client's business, or because the client has not honestly expressed personal expectations that are more important than stated objectives.

- Big guns often fire blanks. Determine who has the experience, who will do your work and who will be accountable. PR agencies, especially the big ones, have a business model of presenting the "big guns" during new business presentations and then handing the work off to junior staff once they win your business. On the other hand, a senior-level communications sole practitioner with deep credentials, vast contacts, savvy approaches and a network of similar professionals with complimentary skills might be far more beneficial than a so-called full-service global agency in creating the results you need.

- Chemistry. Chemistry with the communications team is important; it will lead to results. I suppose it is not unlike dating. While I researched the factors in finding the right agency match, Barbara Robinson at Dun and Bradstreet said it best: "Chemistry between the agency and the internal team … will the agency be fun to work with? PR is hard work so why not make the hard work fun?"

- Gut sense. Rely on your intuition to judge what people say and how they conduct themselves.

- Top-quality strategic communications strategists. Partner with people who know competitive trends, take pride in accomplishing terrific results for their clients and are authentic professionals in their field. Invest in the talent of such professionals, and you will enjoy outstanding results. After all, you are entrusting them to successfully enhance the image, reputation and brand of your organization.

- Strategic communications consultants are not simply vendors. The people who supply your office with computers, IT services and coffee machines are vendors. To position your organization competitively, and to become even more successful, invest in smart communications pros with clever ideas.

Consider a bold new direction. Take charge. Set tough expectations for an agency, if you have one. Better yet, beef up your own communications team with world-class expertise. It's not difficult to go out and hire strategic communications pros and former journalists who can enhance your organization's brand and bottom line.

Chapter Nine:
Blogging Has Come a Long Way

Back in 2003, when I began to learn the blog world — the blogosphere — and launched my first blog, it was all about personal expression, sort of like standing on a wooden box at Speaker's Corner near Hyde Park in London and shouting out an opinion. But that soon changed with recognition of the nearly limitless interactive and dynamic qualities of the blog platform. It's because of blog technology that the Internet has become alive with video, audio and every type of exchange imaginable.

Blogs today are used for conversations, listening, sharing and exchanges of all kinds of styles. Blog technology drives many of the world's most popular mainstream newspaper Web sites; online media and resource sites; e-commerce; social networks; and microblogging sites, such as Twitter, in addition to tens of millions of independent, personal and stand-alone blogs.

While the Internet started with static HTML code sites, much of the interest has shifted to blog technology.

Data from eMarketer — a leading source for market research and trend analysis on Internet, e-business, online marketing and media — reflects the explosive popularity of blogs:

Among the 199.2 million Internet users in the United States in 2009, nearly one-half, or 48.5 percent, read blogs. That translates into 96.6 million blog readers in the nation, according to eMarketer. Additionally, the company estimates there are 27.9 million bloggers in the United States, with millions more worldwide.

EMarketer concludes that "blogging activity presents new opportunities for marketers to monitor and influence conversations relevant to their businesses ... opportunities no marketer should ignore." Neither should anyone who is in public relations or communications or is the head of an organization.

I referred earlier to the 2009 study on the media, designed by Don Bates, founding director of the master's degree program in strategic public relations at George Washington University in Washington, D.C.

The results of his survey show that more editors and journalists than ever monitor blogs for story ideas. Such a trend presents significant opportunities for businesses or organizations to use blog technology for online newsrooms and become legitimate news resources, not only about their own organizations but to guide the voice and image of entire industries or business sectors.

Imagine, for example, if a hospital known for orthopedics were to develop a blog style online newsroom to showcase an ever-changing spectrum of news and discussions about new medical procedures, in additional to its own attributes and specialties. The hospital's communications people could build awareness and visitors through online social media sites, such as Twitter and Facebook.

The medical facility's image could become known and respected as the go-to place for information and updates about the latest procedures, medical breakthroughs and news. Visibility would grow around the world, aided by being recognized as a credible online information resource. That's one way reputations are built in the digital era.

The blogosphere has exploded with new concepts for sharing information. At the same time, it has spawned a curious mixture of genuine experts and snake oil salesmen.

A local chapter of the International Association of Business Communicators (IABC), an excellent professional organization, unwittingly invited a self-professed "blog guru" from a local public relations agency to speak about latest blogging trends. What they did not know was that the fellow had never started a blog and had never written a blog of his own, even though he was consulting with clients about blogging skills.

I have watched and chuckled with fellow bloggers about the proliferation of so-called blog gurus, but it was not until I became active on Twitter that I realized the scope of such self-proclaimed experts, many of whom have never launched a blog and are fairly new to the environment. Equally endemic is the number of people on Twitter who claim to be social media gurus.

All the bravado becomes a challenge for an organization that simply wants to hire skill and know-how for guidance about the online world. Here are some tips:

- Check credentials, achievements and hands-on experience. Ask for references, send a few e-mails and make some phone calls.

- Popularity on Twitter or Facebook does not necessarily translate into solid credentials. While someone may be a terrific self-promoter, he or she may lack practical experience.

- Seek out similarities for your own project. Find someone who has worked on a project akin to your own.

- Beware of self-proclaimed gurus and experts. In an environment as fast-moving, expansive and changing as the Internet, few people can honestly make such grandiose claims.

- Independent consultants usually have greater experience and knowledge of blogging, social media and the online world than public relations, marketing and advertising agencies. Agencies, by their very financial model and more traditional techniques, have been astonishingly slow to learn Web 2.0.

Not long ago, a large public relations agency approached me for guidance on how to set up a blog for the agency's cofounder. As I sat across a table from the agency's head of technology and other executives, I quietly realized that this agency knew nothing — absolutely nothing — about all the latest developments, not only about blogs but online in general, and how mobile wireless has become such an integral component.

Yet here was a PR agency that was advising its clients about online strategies, a world that they themselves do not fully comprehend. How does this happen? Because most agencies have dispensed with training programs and anything else that might eat into valuable time that can be billed to clients.

For any business or organization, the act of setting up a blog is no big deal. In fact, it has become quite easy. The challenge comes with figuring out what to do with the blog, whether CEO or corporate blog, and asking how it will mesh with the organization's overall strategic vision and purpose.

My experience has found that many corporate blogs — like the ones run by teams of people at Dell Computer — quickly turn into compulsive one-way selling, promotion and hype ... pushing out marketing messages. Such corporate blogs have replaced sales brochures and other marketing materials, together with lack of balance and perspective. I suppose it's natural that when you unleash marketing people on a blog, it will take on the look and feel of an advertisement.

Throughout this book, I have worked to present ideas for developing an organization's reputation with communications approaches that underscore transparency, openness and credibility. In that spirit, let me suggest a more balanced corporate blog style that also helps an organization manage news, extend prominent visibility and be viewed by wider audiences as an expert and trusted information resource:

- You be the expert. Present both sides of the latest developments and news in your business sector or industry, not just your own marketing materials.

- Invite commentary from high-profile thought leaders and experts. Ask analysts, reviewers, researchers, academics and others to contribute balanced articles that will be featured on your corporate blog.

- Present trends. Become among the first to showcase or repost trend research that impacts your industry, even if the source of the research was not your organization.

- Invite conversations and feedback. Use a corporate blog to listen to what people are saying about your industry, your company and you.

- Present your own news. Spotlight the latest news and developments but avoid making the blog a dusty old online "pressroom," like that of so many other organizations. The people who care about your organization, including the media, only want the latest information.

- Enhance visual appeal. Make a corporate blog rich with images, photos and graphs.

Let's now turn to the idea of a CEO blog. If an organization's top executive recognizes the importance of achieving unique differentiation in today's fiercely competitive world, and is willing to roll up his or her sleeves and actively work and invest the time to share the vision of a business or organization through speeches, roundtables, conferences and the media, then a blog might be a natural extension of that strategic outreach initiative. But it requires an investment of time and work.

On the other hand, if a CEO is more insular or uncomfortable getting out in front of his or her organization as a leader, a blog might not be appropriate.

In my consulting work, I believe these are the first questions that must be asked when considering a CEO blog:

- Why? Why have a CEO blog? What is the burning desire to have a blog?

- What's the purpose? What is the objective?

- What's to be achieved by a CEO blog?

- Will the blog be used to listen and exchange ideas, or will it be used to boost brand awareness and increase sales?

Here is a four-step evaluation I use in working with a leader to determine whether a CEO might be appropriate and valuable for interfacing with key audiences. You will notice that the elements are similar to those for a corporate blog:

1. Pledge to resist marketing, selling and promoting. If a CEO (or the organization) wants to use a CEO blog to market, sell and promote through a CEO blog, or if a CEO expects that someone else in the organization will write the blog, or if a CEO only intends to get involved with the blog every couple of weeks or so, then I might strongly recommend against

the whole idea of a CEO blog. Today's online audiences will quickly see through it as contrived or disingenuous. If the corporate marketing or PR departments want to "brand" the look and feel of a CEO blog to be seamless with the rest of the organization, it risks detracting from credibility and transparency.

2. Pledge to be distinctive. I believe a CEO blog should reflect the uniqueness of a CEO's personality. As an example, look at the style of the popular CEO blogs of Zappos' Tony Hsieh, and Mark Cuban's Blog Maverick. A CEO blog is a place where the human side of a CEO is displayed, where ideas and vision are candidly shared. It's a timely and active place where buyers, customers, stakeholders and others can vent frustration, complain or praise directly to the person in charge. It is all out there in the open for everyone to see.

3. Listen. Use a CEO blog to listen to which way the wind is blowing in your marketplace. Listen to buyers and customers. Listen to the media. Listen to opposing ideas, criticism and complaints. Identify opportunities for growth by listening to feedback to a CEO blog.

4. Take genuine action. Consider the importance of a CEO directly interfacing publicly with someone who has a complaint, responding promptly to the concern and taking immediate action to resolve that person's complaint. Engage in conversations and demonstrate affirmative responses. All the people who witness that blog conversation will be left with a positive impression and an inclination to share that positive experience or story with others. It's how the image and reputation of distinctive and authentic leadership is defined and achieved in today's online world.

At the end of the day, blogs are nothing more than tactical, interactive online delivery platforms for sharing ideas. It requires thought and planning to make a blog worthwhile, keeping in mind that the whole concept of blogging continues to evolve at amazing speed. The idea of a CEO blog may seem like the right decision today, but what about next year and into the future, as the online environment shifts and changes?

Gary Shapiro of the Consumer Electronics Association, whom I mentioned earlier, told me that he questions the benefits of CEO blogs as a way of getting attention because CEOs do not read the blogs of other CEOs. He makes a valid point. Blogging for blogging's sake or to impress peers is a waste of time.

Blogging in business or industry must have a purpose. One needs first to consider the overall realistic goals of a CEO blog or the concept of corporate blogging. Businesses need to have measurable and achievable goals for every activity they engage in, and that includes investing the time in blogging and the expected outcomes.

While I am a proponent of corporate blogging, blogs should have the same responsibility as any other Web page on an organization's site: attract and engage visitors, hopefully converting them to the next step in a relationship.

When employees are given the freedom and job safety to blog about specific areas of their own expertise, blogs tend to be more credible in the role of engaging and developing interactive conversations with an organization's audiences and customers. It is at that point when customers may start thinking, "Hey, these guys really know their business, and they care about what I have to say!"

I use the words "freedom" and "job safety" for a reason. The risk of misstatement, even unintended innuendo, is enormous on a blog. If an organization encourages employees to express their personal expertise on a blog and to voice opinions about the company openly, then top executives must accept that not everything said will be rosy and perfectly in step with what corporate leaders hope for as far as the image of their organization. Well-meaning employees should not be in jeopardy if their employer disagrees with their opinions written on a company-backed blog.

When employees have complete job security from their bosses to blog, the payoff ultimately will be enhanced corporate credibility and respect among stakeholders. Quite frankly, I believe that employee blogging can be a good way to build online brand awareness by creating word of mouth about your organization.

The safety net for CEO blogging, however, is somewhat trickier and could become a slippery slope. Let me explain.

Suppose you, as leader of an organization, have started a blog at the urging of the PR and marketing people to better promote your leadership image. And one day something really ticks you off. Perhaps a reporter has said something you didn't like, and you feel the need to write a few words about it publicly on the blog. The headache then begins because you have potentially presented a negative or controversial image of yourself and your organization.

There is a time and a place for everything, and CEO blogs are not the forum to respond to insults or attacks.

The executive director of a trade association in Washington, D.C., decided to have a blog, and it ultimately cost him his job. When he posted a personal rant about a controversial issue facing his organization, his board of directors asked him to step down from his position. His blog got him fired.

Remember, blogs are merely communications tools and must be used with skill and common sense. Furthermore, there are savvier and safer ways to boost your image and that of your organization.

We are still missing the point that in today's intensely competitive world, the core responsibility of strategic communications is to create authentic competitive differentiation, using fresh and imaginative ways that will deliver meaningful and tangible results.

If you are leading an organization, it is far more important to focus on clear and accurate messages to capture an audience's attention and the interest of reporters.

Are we running the risk that technology will make the practice of public relations even more insular? Will all the gadgets of the digital revolution merely act as a crutch so we can avoid talking to each other and the press and target audiences? In our breathless rush to new styles of media online, are we perpetuating a troubling copycat technology trend in PR?

And most worrisome, is PR hoping that by creating and manipulating its own image of online media, we can ignore our failures for having the legitimate contacts and knowing how to work with the real journalists at the mainstream news media?

The warning signs are already out there. So is an astonishing spectrum of new opportunities. Perhaps the solution is for true leaders and communicators to improve their own skills in the admittedly imperfect craft of online communications, and then to consider which new tactics are appropriate for reaching out to clients, and which are not. There are still many agencies practicing a style of PR today that became obsolete years ago.

Chapter Ten:
Untangling Online Strategies and Web 2.0

Why should a leader or executive care about the online digital communications strategy of his or her organization? Why bother? What's the importance and the return on investment?

The answer is easy: everything. The future of most organizations today depends on effective online communications, the transparency of their messages matched with the methods of online communications and how well they listen to and engage their audiences.

It is no longer pushing information at audiences or even being interactive. We must now seek personal conversations with audiences if we are to identify opportunities and respond to new trends.

Online communications technology has become a powerful force of change and collaboration within organizations. It enhances brand awareness and reputation management. It defines authentic leadership.

Visitors to Web sites today often make snap judgments about whether they are attracted to an organization or not, based solely on an impression or perception of how the organization presents itself online. Visitors may ask themselves, "Is this someone I wish to do business with?" If an organization's Web site sends murky, ambiguous or rambling messages, the downside can be serious.

Today, any company or organization has the ability to help chart the future — through the clarity and transparency of its messages and how it utilizes the expanding spectrum of Web 2.0 online communications tools.

Web 2.0 is a new generation and evolving trend in World Wide Web technology and online design, helping organizations not only interface more effectively with their audiences but also take communications to the level of personal conversation. The tools of Web 2.0 include blogs and dynamic content management sites that are an offshoot of blog technology, wikis or online collaborative sharing of knowledge, podcasts, video and social networking sites such as Yelp, Facebook and Twitter.

Web 2.0 and the multitude of new services and products it brings, like Wordpress, are revolutionizing how many organizations communicate with their employees, shareholders, customers, the media and partners through instantaneous sharing of information.

The CEO of an organization now has the ability, for example, to take the pulse of his or her company, engage employees in conversations directly and receive candid and unbiased feedback and ideas through personal internal blog conversations, without filtering through divisional level managers. Leaders can use the communications technology of Web 2.0 to both speak and listen with greater clarity, which ultimately will lead to better productivity, competitive advantages and enhanced brand.

At Cisco Systems, Jeanette Gibson is director of new media within corporate communications at Cisco Systems, a global company built on a culture of looking into the future of communication among people, communities, governments and businesses worldwide. Her job is to embrace and help define the future of online communications. It's also her passion, and few people I have spoken with see into the dynamic future of the exciting convergence of communications, information and technology with greater clarity and leadership.

With the Internet's openness and transparency and all of an organization's information out for the public to view, Gibson says it's important to look at how you are viewed externally and whether that is the brand you want to showcase.

It's critical for executives to be involved in an organization's online strategy, Gibson says. At Cisco Systems, for example, senior executives, including CEO John Chambers, are engaged with blogging and doing podcasts because they are finding that it helps them to better connect with audiences, trends and immediate marketplace fluctuations. More important to the organization's image and reputation, these leaders give voice, face and personality to a major corporation, and that equates to enhanced trust and connection with essential audiences.

It's inexpensive, she underscores, to roll out these tools of Web 2.0, and an executive need not be a technology expert to post and engage in personal online conversations with members of key audiences.

I asked Gibson to look into the future and share her advice to media-savvy leaders on how to take charge of their own organization's online strategy, using the tools of Web 2.0:

- Consider your organization's culture. What is acceptable, and what is your tolerance for risk? Any new media program involves a sense of recognizing that you are no longer fully in control, a big challenge for many executives.

- Accept that we all are doing business in a new world. The landscape has changed. Doing business today requires a sense of transparency and new ways of engaging customers, employees, stakeholders and other important audiences.

- Adapt technology to extend your distinct needs. Business-to-business, business-to-consumers, not-for-profits, government and NGOs need to customize online communications and the tools of Web 2.0 to achieve their own unique voice and brand image.

- Listen, watch and monitor what's online about your organization. Recognize that what might be said about your organization on a social networking site might impact everything from recruiting new employees to brand image.

- Examine how your organization packages information. In the past, an organization might have just issued a press release. Today's communication trends require a careful look at messages, the kind of medium that can be used to enhance messages, how the information can be brought to life visually, and how online technology can be used to tell a more appealing story to a broader spectrum of audiences.

- Actively practice storytelling to bring your organization's messages and communications to life. For example, the headline of a Cisco news release reads CISCO GATHERS GLOBAL LEADERS TO EXPLORE HOW TECHNOLOGY CAN TRANSFORM APPROACH TO

ENVIRONMENTAL CONCERNS, SUSTAINABILITY AND ECONOMIC DEVELOPMENT. The headline itself is captivating, positions the company as a leader and is a ready-made story that can be communicated effectively via nearly any tool of Web 2.0. For this event, the company's communications included a Webcast, blogging, podcasts, visuals and corporate Web site support, together with the more traditional PR approaches.

Leadership online requires some risk. There is the reality of learning that not everyone loves your personality or your organization. But there is also the direct chance of turning around a negative opinion and making a friend. Executive blogging requires time and attention each day in order to establish a conversation of credibility with audiences.

Even major public relations agencies have a lot to learn about the changing styles, dynamics, methods, and influence of the tools of Web 2.0. A few of the smart ones are scrambling to learn.

Blogging and podcasting by leaders should not be delegated if you wish to achieve any level of trust and candor. An executive can never hope to build a dialogue by posting on a blog every couple of months. Blogging is a daily discipline of not only expressing opinion but also of listening and establishing conversation.

Gibson underscores that the rise of social media and Web 2.0 is a strategic advantage for companies to better communicate, engage, collaborate and respond to tomorrow's opportunities.

Knowledge of how to leverage and utilize the rapid convergence of communications, information and Web 2.0 technologies will define tomorrow's leaders.

PART 2
Get in the Game. Make a Difference.

Chapter Eleven:
Each of Us Has a Voice

The rising popularity of the Internet has made us all more aware of events that impact our lives and the world around us. When news happens, whether down the street or on another continent, it is often reported first by someone online, perhaps using a blog or social media site. A sea change in how information is shared, it is having a profound impact on the ages-old definition of journalism and the media.

Who is a journalist in today's changing world, and how can we in the business of strategic communications better connect and communicate with them?

The answers involve learning new techniques. But we need to move quickly, and we have a lot to learn. It begins by letting go of the bygone notion that anyone in the news media is influenced by traditional PR tactics, such as shoveling press materials at the media or hiding behind prepared remarks.

The media today, and what is interpreted as journalism, is dramatically different than it was when this century began just several years ago.

An event that instigated an online revolution, known today as "citizen journalism," happened in late 2004, when a tsunami roared over islands and populated coastal areas in Asia and East Africa, killing tens of thousands of people without warning. Dramatic video images of the sea devouring whole communities, which aired on television news around the world, were taken mostly by tourists, not TV news crews, who were lucky enough to be in higher locations, and who had the presence of mind to pick up their digital cameras and shoot.

The second event was the series of terrorist bombings in London, England, on July 7, 2005, and the third was Hurricane Katrina, which devastated New Orleans, La., and the Gulf Coast.

Each event had the effect of creating a new type of journalist: "Citizen journalists," ordinary people like you and me who are witnesses to news in the making. These events shook up mainstream and online media news organizations and forced them to recognize that the forces of news, technology and reality have altered the face of journalism forever.

For anyone who seeks to attract and control the media's attention, the events presented new opportunities and new methods of communicating more influentially than ever through the media. Strategic communications methods are evolving seemingly at light speed. The message is clear: Stop mailing out all those news releases and watch the trends.

When the July 7 bombs detonated in the London tube, eyewitness video — the only video available of the explosions — was taken by passengers who switched their mobile phones to video mode and took dramatic pictures. When editors at BBC Television News became aware of the grainy yet spellbinding video, they immediately made the decision to put those images on the air as quickly as possible. The riveting video was broadcast around the world, driving home the horror of terrorism for many of us.

"The London bombs of 7/7 changed the business of broadcast news forever," Jon Williams, a senior editor at BBC Television News, wrote me in an e-mail interview. "For the first time, the audience became 'citizen journalists' en masse by sending their mobile phone pictures — stills and video — by SMS [cell phone text messaging] and e-mail.

"Potentially everyone is a journalist. If something goes wrong — if something happens — someone, somewhere, will capture it on a mobile phone (or video or digital camera)."

Within hours of the July 7 bombings, the BBC was alerting viewers and listeners about special Internet links where witnesses could upload any pictures or video they had captured. Response was overwhelming, and the venerable British news institution quickly found their coverage ahead of competitors, all because their viewers had become their reporters.

It is my personal observation that this almost instant partnership between an audience and the BBC speaks volumes about citizens' devotion to and respect for the news operations of the British

Broadcasting Corporation. It is a loyalty that today eludes television news organizations in the United States, partly because there are far more choices for getting news in America.

There's a larger reason for the audience disenfranchisement in the United States. So many broadcast news outfits in America, which focus on delivering entertainment- and formula-driven news, have isolated themselves from what is relevant and meaningful in their respective communities and from their audiences.

As many media relations specialists know all too well, it's often a challenge to reach the right person at a TV or radio newsroom. For the average citizen, who may have a legitimate news story but lacks the unlisted telephone numbers or e-mail address, it's nearly impossible. So, while the local eyewitness news may promote themselves as "on your side" and "working harder for you," they have not, in all honesty, worked to reach out and earn the loyalty of their audiences. That isolationist behavior by broadcast newsrooms is beginning to turn around out of necessity for survival.

A couple of months after the terrorist bombings in London, an enormous hurricane named Katrina struck the Gulf Coast and the city of New Orleans. The devastation was beyond comprehension. As fierce winds blew and the storm surge leveled towns along the coast, amateur photographers, armed with their small video and digital still cameras, normally intended for home movies and pictures of the family and vacations, captured effects of the historic storm.

What caught my attention during the Katrina disaster was the openness of the news media to accepting visual coverage from ordinary folks, like you and me. Even if you were a public relations person who had outstanding and relevant video of a news event, the media would likely be open to airing your pictures with full knowledge that you might be working to promote a client.

During examples of political revolution — such as in aftermath of the controversial and disputed 2009 presidential election in Iran, as I have written earlier — the Internet has become an essential tool for sharing news, information and video instantly around the world.

A dynamic woman named Shoba Purushothaman is at the forefront of defining what a part of the future of television news may look like using the Internet and how video will be shared. What she sees will be transparent, truthful and fast moving.

Purushothaman is founder and chief executive officer of The News Market,[34] a New York-based company that describes itself as using the latest "Web technology to facilitate easy and efficient transfers of broadcast-standard digital video and other multimedia content from providers to journalists."

From my experience in television news, I would describe The News Market as a tactical digital platform that handles the logistics and technology of getting your video before a vast universe of traditional and online media while you focus on strategy and messages. It is an online distributor of news video and editorial content from the business and nonprofit world.

The old-fashioned style of distributing video news releases to local TV newsrooms via expensive satellite services is on its way out. News video today is distributed far more economically and faster as online digital file transfers to broadcast TV, bloggers and even newspapers. The process has become quick, easy and fairly affordable.

With technical support facilities in her native India and in China, Purushothaman's The News Market is growing at a rate of 80 to 100 percent each year, distributing news video on behalf of clients that range from Airbus, Volvo, Nokia and Adidas to the Red Cross, the World Bank and UNICEF.

Purushothaman says her clients are organizations that recognize there are no boundaries anymore from a business perspective. She envisions a future news environment where traditional news hierarchies and middlemen will vaporize and organizations will have the ability to communicate their news directly to consumers, without intermediaries.

Whether it comes to that or not, we truly live in a flat global communications world today — as Thomas L. Friedman wrote in his best seller *The World is Flat* — and the whole business of communicating news is being rethought, recalibrated and reinvented. Breaking news in one market can instantly impact something around the world, and organizations need to be on alert and know how to use the latest tools of the new style of online media to protect their brands and accurately deliver messages.

---

[34] www.thenewsmarket.com

Chapter Twelve:
Communications with Impact

A current challenge for communicators and decision makers at businesses and organizations is how to build more awareness online while still reaching out to traditional or mainstream media channels, even though they are dwindling. Such a goal is not difficult to achieve … so long as an organization is willing to try new things, and that includes getting outside its comfort space.

Communications in the digital era has markedly expanded our horizon of opportunities. Strategic communications that maximizes impact in today's instant, digital media world is more accountable and can achieve more impressive results than ever before … but only when an organization hires exceptional leaders with experience, and then gives them a seat at the decision-making table. Equate what you want accomplished versus what you think it is worth. Avoid the temptation to cheap it out.

Do research within and outside your organization to frankly determine the value of your objectives. What is the value of enhancing and protecting your brand and reputation? Examine not only how you would like your organization seen and talked about, but also the reality of who you are. Look at shining examples within your own industry, if any, and then hire solid communications professionals with authentic and deep credentials.

Most of all, when you hire outstanding communicators, be open to the new ideas they bring … and ready to consider the changes and improvements they suggest.

Let me share an example of opposites. Apple and Dell both make computers, yet Dell's internal PR efforts are more old school, while

Apple's corporate communications team is the best, in my opinion, of any on the planet, regardless of industry. Dell hires several agencies in hopes of getting PR expertise the company lacks in-house; Apple does not hire outside agencies but invests in assembling a staff with extensive skills. Apple's communications team is easily accessible; Dell's is not.

Here's a little test that I actually tried. Let's pretend I was a general assignment reporter at a daily newspaper. My editor asked me to contact both Apple and Dell to ask some questions for a story because the paper's technology reporter was on vacation. I was under a deadline, and I had no contacts at either company. My first task would be to check the companies' respective Web sites.

At the bottom of Apple's home page,[35] I clicked Media Info and was taken to a Media Resources page, where I found everything I needed — all the names, e-mail addresses, telephone numbers and areas of responsibility of every Apple corporate communications employee. I found all the contact information and could make a call to the right person at Apple within 30 seconds.

Dell's Web site[36] was another story. I clicked CONTACT at the bottom of the home page, but there was nothing about media contacts. So, I had to go fishing, and I clicked SITE MAP. There, I found PRESS ROOM, but when I clicked on it, there were no references to specific contacts for the news media staff. There was only a generic form that I could fill out, with this caveat: "The press line is staffed from 8 a.m. to 6 p.m. Central Time, Monday through Friday." I completed the form but never heard back from anyone at Dell.

Dell has what I would label an old-fashioned PR department. Apple, on the other hand, has a media-savvy team. Now, I have a question for you: Which kind of communications department does your organization have?

It's not surprising that Apple greatly overshadows Dell when it comes to capturing headlines, publicity buzz and superb media stories. All the media attention that Apple generates creates what marketing people call "the halo effect," because the payoff is directly seen in higher sales and shareholder value.

---

[35] www.apple.com
[36] www.dell.com

When Apple debuts a new laptop, it makes headlines; Dell, however, relies largely on paid advertising and a press release that reads similar to previous ones. Apple's dominance of coverage in both today's mainstream and new online media eclipses Dell's efforts, which are quite simply feeble by comparison. Apple's sales, growing market share and customer satisfaction reflect the success.

There is also little doubt about which company is the more dynamic brand and visionary market leader in the future of technology. Certainly paid advertising helps, but today's most exciting and influential strategic initiatives are driven by outstanding strategic communications that reach out and engage all audiences primarily online, from customers and stakeholders to the media.

There is an important trend happening today as more and more organizations recognize the importance and value of clearly communicating vision with greater influence by generating outstanding news media coverage: A growing number of today's most successful organizations are making the investment in beefing up their communications team in-house rather than gambling to hire outside help.

Look closely at the organizations led by Steve Jobs of Apple, Gary Shapiro at the Consumer Electronics Association, and others, and you will see top-notch communications teams on staff. From the perspective of these leaders, an in-house team knows the workings of their own organizations, the competitive landscape, the authentic story that needs to be communicated and the visionary leadership of the person at the helm better than any outside agency or consultant. The contacts and relationships they forge with journalists are invaluable.

The payoff benefits to these organizations are significant, ranging from a greatly enhanced level of accountability to delivering brand awareness and excitement to broad and diverse audiences and increased shareholder value. Sounds like a smart investment to me.

Chapter Thirteen:
Crisis Never Takes a Day Off

When I was an on-air correspondent for CBS News, I witnessed how many organizations reacted in crisis. It was usually a fumbling manner that fell into one of three different yet predictable styles:

1. Pull down the shades, turn out the lights, say nothing, pretend it will go away and discuss changing the name of the company.

2. Have a spokesperson or, even worse, lawyer read a prepared statement admitting no guilt or involvement, passing the blame and pledging to cooperate with unspecified authorities to the fullest extent, while really having no intention to do so.

3. Have the CEO stand up in front of a battery of microphones and blame the press for intruding on the crisis, a behavior usually reserved for CEOs of mining companies during underground disasters.

Things haven't changed much over the years, by the way, for many organizations when they have a crisis. Such conduct sends a message that an organization has not bothered to invest in advance crisis preparedness, is not interested in openness or transparency and suggests a perception of guilt because we have all seen it too often before.

Times have changed. Even though we still occasionally see defensiveness by an organization with a problem, it has become not only ineffective but also counterproductive and possibly injurious to an organization's image and brand reputation.

Amazon.com[37] found itself suddenly in the middle of the media's spotlight and harsh criticism for delisting from its sales ranking system gay and lesbian book titles that someone deemed to be "adult." It happened over a weekend, and the news rocketed around the world via Twitter, blogs and other online social media at a time when no one at Amazon apparently was monitoring news about the company. Consider the irony of an online company failing to monitor breaking news online about itself.

Amazon characterized the action at first as a mistake, a software glitch. But the online and media controversy failed to subside, and by the time the company's communications people finally comprehended the extent of the crisis, nearly a week had elapsed.

Any delay in addressing crisis communications in the digital age can be damaging to an organization's reputation. In today's online world, several days are an eternity.

We are all living in a new era of openness, timeliness, responsiveness and truthfulness. The media environment has truly become 24/7. Adverse publicity and inaccurate information can spin out of control in an instant. Any organization's best defense is smart preparation:

- Develop and maintain an interactive online newsroom — an authentic news information resource, including such elements as specific contact information for media representatives, timely news updates and relevant industry specific materials.

- Recognize that today's news cycle is all the time. Assign staff to watch for any news about the organization through basic free services such as Google Alerts.

- Respond with lightning speed. Monitor for the first sign of adverse publicity or media coverage. This need not be time-consuming; it can be as quick as reading a Google Alert on a mobile wireless device, like an iPhone or BlackBerry.

---

[37] www.amazon.com

- Accept that the "media" can have many faces. Respond to a question from a blogger with the same timeliness and respect as a question from a mainstream media reporter.

We want to see leaders in front of the cameras, expressing genuine sincerity and compassion. We want to hear them talking to us even if they don't know the full story but are doing everything possible to make things right and will keep us updated. And we expect a believable tone of compassion in their voices.

While the need is always there for an organization to put together a common sense plan for the eventuality of a crisis, Web 2.0 has changed crisis response in the world of public relations from wooden-sounding "announcements," or talking at audiences, into more productive "conversations" and listening.

Forget the old days of Mike Wallace of CBS *60 Minutes* kicking in the door with his camera crew behind him. That never really happened, anyway, even though it has become folklore in the corporate world, where many CEOs still fear and detest the media, often for reasons of lack of credibility that they personally created.

An organization today is more likely to be scalded and damaged by bloggers and adverse buzz on social media sites, and far more quickly than by what's left of the traditional mainstream news media. Many newspapers are operating on a fraction of the staff they had a year ago — that is, if the newspaper is still in business. Network and cable television news are utilizing interns to cut costs. So when a crisis happens, chances are good that a mainstream news reporter will hear about it first from a blogger or an online social media site, like Twitter. It's a fact in the world we live in.

The new mandate in crisis communications is openness, transparency, timeliness and engaging stakeholders, customers, employees, the media and, especially, bloggers and online news services that cover any industry or organization. There is no longer such a thing as a "secret." At the same time, a "no comment" or a slow comment may drive a dagger through the heart of an organization's reputation.

Chapter Fourteen:
Working in the World's Spotlight

Sometimes a strategic communications assignment in support of an issue or cause is so immense, intricate and controversial on a global scale that the only way to tackle it is to reach out for help among acquaintances in the media.

It was the spring of 2002, and emotions in America were still raw from the terrorist attacks of 9/11. The Bush administration had responded by sending troops to Afghanistan to seek out the proclaimed masterminds of the attacks, including Osama bin Laden and ostensibly any of the other bad guys.

United States warplanes were bombing the country "back to the Stone Ages," administration pundits crowed. It was before the shift of attention to Iraq after bin Laden proved to be too difficult and too elusive to capture.

The White House had succeeded in convincing much of the country and many journalists that it was making the correct responses, and those actions included herding up hundreds of possible "suspects" and incarcerating them.

Those men — whom Vice President Dick Cheney was calling "the worst of the worst" even before the United States knew anything about any of them — were first held in crowded detention stockades in Pakistan and Afghanistan. Many were stripped and beaten or sprayed with cold water from hoses for long periods. Then most were flown, stripped naked and hog-tied in inhuman positions on the cold bare metal floors of U.S. cargo planes, to a newly cobbled together prison at the Unites States base of Guantánamo, on the island of Cuba, where they were held as enemy combatants.

The term "enemy combatants" had been concocted by the White House legal staff as a way to get around the law and to permit the Unites States to detain indefinitely anyone they did not like.

For all many of us knew, these so-called enemy combatants were some of the terrorists who had attacked our country on 9/11. The White House told us so.

What many of us did not fully comprehend at that time was that White House attorneys believed they had found a way to circumvent the Constitution, Bill of Rights, Geneva Convention and all domestic and international laws pertaining to human rights and due process. By using the label of enemy combatant and through establishing a network of off-shore prisons, suspects could be held and interrogated for as long as the administration wanted. The White House wanted to block the suspects from access to attorneys, to their families and to the outside world. Most of all, they wanted to prevent access to U.S. courts.

Early that April 2002, I had a call from Thomas Wilner, a prominent international human rights and trade attorney in Washington, D.C. He wanted to meet to discuss my potential help on a case he had just taken on — the plight of twelve Kuwaiti men believed to be detained at Guantánamo — and his plans to file a lawsuit against the Bush administration's intentions to deny the men of due process rights. The chairman of a public relations agency in Washington had referred me to Wilner, saying his agency could not touch something so controversial, especially so soon after 9/11.

A day later, I was in Wilner's law offices on Pennsylvania Avenue, which looked out at the United States Capitol. He explained that the families of the Kuwaiti 12 had hired him through an intermediary law firm in Kuwait. He was to determine the fate of their loved ones. Wilner had sought out a communications strategist with connections to support planned litigation, and to manage what he anticipated would become significant potential media interest. His instincts about media interest turned out to be accurate.

During the initial meeting, we identified a primary task: to draft several clear, credible and accurate talking points or messages to help everyone involved speak as one voice, consistently from the same page.

We also agreed that the issue we were facing was not one of discussing or even speculating on the guilt or innocence of anyone because we knew so little about the 12 men. Besides that, guilt or innocence was irrelevant. The key issue, and the reason I accepted the assignment, was the denial of human rights and due process of law as afforded by the Constitution and the rule of law in our country.

Within a few days, I was on a flight to Kuwait to meet with the families, as Wilner had done just a week earlier, and try to piece together information about the 12 men so we could begin to get a picture of what we were facing. We agreed to compare notes upon my return.

During meetings with the family members in Kuwait, I intentionally and naturally fell into a journalist style of asking questions and then asking a similar question using different words to probe deeper for information, listen and take copious notes.

I learned that many of the Kuwaitis had been captured not on any battlefield in or near Afghanistan, but in Pakistan while working individually on a variety of human rights efforts. It is a legacy among Kuwaitis, who are often more affluent than others in the Middle East, to assist with money and their own labor on agricultural projects and to build schools and mosques in neighboring regions.

For example, one detainee, Fouad Mahmoud Al Rabiah, was in his 40s, an aviation engineer with an established career at Kuwaiti Airlines and the father of four children. He had graduated from Embry-Riddle Aeronautical University and was granted honorary citizenship by the Daytona Beach, Fla., Chamber of Commerce. He had volunteered to work on a rescue campaign in Kosovo in 1988.

Another, Fayiz Mohammed Ahmed Al Kandari, was a university student who had traveled to Afghanistan during summer vacation prior to 9/11. It was his belief that helping others might honor his grandmother, who had just died, and bring better health to his mother, who was suffering from cancer.

Fawzi Khaled Al Odah, a schoolteacher in his 20s, had spent summers traveling in poor nations to educate less fortunate students. He had been caught in the turmoil in Pakistan after the extensive United States bombings and search for bin Laden in neighboring Afghanistan, and he had simply been in the wrong place at the wrong time, swept up like many other men by U.S. forces because he looked out of place.

Fawzi was the son of my host in Kuwait, Khalid Al-Odah. Khalid would become the international face and voice on behalf of the plight of the Kuwaiti detainees at Guantánamo, and he would eventually do hundreds of interviews over the years we worked together with members of the media around the world.

Khalid loved America. A retired Kuwait Air Force colonel who had been trained by the United States Air Force in Arizona, he had fought alongside U.S. forces in Operation Desert Storm in 1991. When we first met in April 2002, he was in a state of disbelief that the United States would indiscriminately hold his son while making no attempt to determine his innocence.

At that time, in the spring of 2002, the U.S. had not yet gotten around to learning anything about the 12 Kuwaitis but held them anyway, along with about 600 other men, in Guantánamo, in what increasingly appeared to be at least partly a PR stunt to reassure the American people that some of the bad people responsible for 9/11 were locked up.

It was better for those guys to be in cells and under guard in a Guantánamo prison than to be bombing the streets of U.S. cities, according to the spin out of the White House and Pentagon, even though no one knew who they were or who was possibly innocent.

The story that attracted my attention during meetings in Kuwait, and that I believed could potentially capture the media's interest as well, were the reports, unconfirmed at that point, of bounty hunting and betrayal involving a U.S. operation that underscored the arbitrary nature of military sweeps to catch possible suspects.

During the intense and widespread bombing of Afghanistan in early 2002, U.S. forces were directed by the Pentagon to pay financial bounties to villagers in Pakistan, near the Afghan border, to betray any strangers they saw in the area.

American forces dropped leaflets that said, essentially, *Turn in a strange-looking Arab and get paid by the United States and feed your family for life.*

It was not a strategic or incisive search for possible terrorists, or even for bin Laden. Quite the contrary: U.S. forces were simply under orders to indiscriminately apprehend as many Arabs as possible. That is what the troops — young American men and women — were ordered to do. Their commanders said they were doing their part to catch bad guys.

Returning to Washington, Wilner and I regrouped, compared notes and got to work. We framed a few talking points that would become the basis for media interviews:

- Just because our country was viciously attacked without warning is not justification to ignore our Constitution, Bill of Rights and laws of our land.

- We are the world's symbol of freedom and should, as a nation, behave better than this. Yet creating an offshore prison to deny basic human rights is wrong and makes us no better than the worst.

- By denying access to due process of law, we are actually putting all Americans abroad, including our troops, in harm's way because we have disregarded rules of the Geneva Conventions on fair treatment.

Upon those few messages, written in plain language, powerful interviews were delivered with focus and clarity. Regardless of breaking news, our central talking points worked and endured over several years and hundreds of interviews.

The next challenge was to find someone in the media who might listen. Quite frankly, my concern was that no one might want to discuss the plight of some Kuwaitis held at Guantánamo because the Bush administration had worked to convince America that everyone held there was guilty of something.

My first call was to an old acquaintance at National Public Radio, Scott Simon, the popular long-time anchor of NPR's Weekend Edition. Simon is widely respected for his integrity and strong sense of fairness. He suggested that I contact NPR's then-legal affairs correspondent Barbara Bradley Hagerty.

One call was all it took to get her attention. Hagerty's interest centered around the legal issue of arbitrary denial of due process of law to avoid certain rights afforded by the United States Constitution. She sensed correctly that it would become a big issue.

Over the next year, she reported numerous developments in the case of the 12 Kuwaitis, including a lengthy interview with Khalid Al-Odah.

While National Public Radio was open to balanced reporting on the Guantánamo situation, that wasn't the case at the *Washington Post*. After an initial meeting with a reporter resulted in a brief story on the

Kuwaitis, the reporter quietly told us that his editors had prohibited further coverage on the subject. We were not surprised. The *Post* was one of several news organizations to be intimidated by the White House during those times, and even today it is struggling to regain its reputation as a meaningful news organization.

Aside from the courageous reporting on National Public Radio, not many journalists wanted to touch a story about detainees at Guantánamo. That all changed when Wilner and I met with Roy Gutman, then a correspondent at *Newsweek*.

Gutman had been awarded the 1993 Pulitzer Prize for stories revealing the horrors of ethnic warfare in the former Yugoslavia, and he was keenly interested in how a U.S. military sweep in Pakistan after 9/11, based on bounty and betrayal, had led to the indiscriminate capture of several of the Kuwaiti detainees.

Working with *Newsweek* staff in Pakistan, Gutman confirmed the U.S. Arab-for-bounty program, and he even got his hands on several of the leaflets that promised enough money to feed a family for life in exchange for turning in an Arab. His team of reporters also confirmed early reports of prisoner mistreatment by U.S. troops.

Gutman's extensive cover story dominated an issue of *Newsweek* in the early summer of 2002, significantly stimulating questions about the propriety of U.S. actions with regard to Guantánamo.

Between Gutman's piece in Newsweek and Bradley Hagerty's continued coverage on National Public Radio, the tide shifted dramatically throughout the news media. All of a sudden, reporters were calling and e-mailing from around the country and from news organizations around the world.

Coverage of the plight of the 12 Kuwaitis who were held incommunicado at Guantánamo became widespread among the Associated Press, BBC News, the *Newark Star-Ledger*, CBS' *60 Minutes*, Agence France-Presse, CNN, *ABC World News Tonight*, *CBS Evening News*, the *Orlando Sentinel*, the *Miami Herald*, the *New York Times*, the *International Herald Tribune* and so on. But not at the *Washington Post*.

Journalists were interested in both the human rights angle and new developments as Wilner and his legal team argued the case through the federal courts on the way to the United States Supreme Court.

When reporters who were new to the story contacted us, they generally wanted to know what other respected journalists had written about the Kuwaiti detainees.

We launched and actively updated a Web site — KuwaitiDetainees.org (now offline) — to present background information about the Kuwaiti 12. The Web site became a critical component in our media outreach campaign.

When reporters want to tackle a story with a sometimes edgy angle, like that of the Kuwaiti detainees, it is helpful for them to have a way to easily point to what other news organizations have reported on the subject when getting clearance from their editors to proceed. The Web site, which we got online within two days, worked perfectly to validate the importance of our story among a growing corps of journalists worldwide.

Content on KuwaitiDetainees.org changed each day, with fresh updates and extensive background information on the legal case, including copies of legal briefs, plus background and photos of the Kuwaiti detainees; contact information to help journalists reach us anytime, day or night; and the growing number of hyperlinks to the extensive media coverage, listed by news organization and date. Traffic to the site soared.

Within a few months, nearly every meaningful news organization in the world had reported the story about the 12 Kuwaiti detainees at Guantánamo. Perhaps even more important, coverage of the whole issue of unjust imprisonment of hundreds of men and denial of human rights by U.S. policy and actions at Guantánamo had become a global story.

I wish I could end this story on a happy note and report that our team helped achieve the expeditious release of the 12 men. I wish I could share with you that we were successful with all the lawsuits and news coverage.

Yet even after years of incarceration for the people at Guantánamo, Vice President Cheney was still out making fundraising speeches before wealthy Republicans, claiming that the prisoners were "the worst of the worst" terrorists, even though no charges were filed.

In the end, it required new leadership in the United States — the administration of President Barack Obama — to eventually take steps to do away with America's embarrassing "black hole." All the while, the Kuwaiti 12 never had their timely day in court.

There was one significant benefit of all the efforts on behalf of the Kuwaiti 12: It sparked heightened world attention over the issue of fundamental human rights during times of global terrorism, stimulating debates over the propriety of denial of due process, inappropriate treatment of prisoners and how far a government can go to skirt its own Constitution and world law.

Chapter Fifteen:
Awareness That Saves Lives

Leaders of not-for-profit organizations frequently tell me that they struggle to get much-needed attention from the news media even when they think they have a good story to tell. Their communications people send out a news release, sometimes using costly press release distribution services, and nothing happens. Their public relations people make media calls, and they are greeted only by voicemail and no calls are returned.

All too often, a nonprofit organization works against itself when it attempts to get the media's attention with outdated methods. Reporters have told me about unreasonable delays when they contact nonprofits, and a lack of understanding about what makes for a timely and meaningful story. Materials are sometimes exaggerated, grammatically incorrect or not factual.

Media coverage is so important to one Washington-based nonprofit that the organization's board and several major funders circumvented the executive director and established mandated "deliverables," or goals, for the communications staff, including issuing a predetermined number of press releases and targeting a specific number of stories to appear in the media.

That example is an impossible and dysfunctional scenario, a surefire recipe for failure. Such arbitrary and naïve objectives cannot be achieved; this further underscores that making news for an organization must never be manipulated by a funder, board member, human resources person, legal department or strategic planner.

Pulling off media coverage in the world of nonprofits is a challenge, and the big names — organizations such as the Gates Foundation, Pew

Charitable Trusts, Habitat for Humanity, Amnesty International — seem to get most of the attention. But others capture the spotlight too, and we see it when leaders take charge and act like leaders.

Let me share the story of one such leader, Layli Miller-Muro, and the organization she founded, the Tahirih Justice Center. Miller-Muro's nonprofit achieves top-quality media stories that directly benefit the organization.

The Tahirih Justice Center is widely respected for providing pro bono legal assistance on behalf of immigrant and refugee women and girls. The issues are often controversial, such as providing legal assistance to women who are seeking asylum or refugee status, particularly from Africa, Asia and the Middle East. Some women are escaping torturous situations, such as female genital mutilation, human trafficking or brutal domestic violence.

Miller-Muro, who is an attorney, founded the center in 1997. While a student in law school, she was involved in a case that made headlines worldwide and led to a dramatic change in how the United States treats victims of gender-based violence who seek asylum. The case did not go well until it caught the media's interest.

Fauziya Kassindja was a 17-year-old girl who fled Togo in fear of a forced polygamous marriage and a tribal practice known as "female genital mutilation." After arriving in the United States and spending more than seventeen months in detention, Ms. Kassindja was granted asylum in 1996 by the United States Board of Immigration Appeals (the highest immigration court) in a decision that opened the door to gender-based persecution as grounds for asylum.

Her case was argued before the immigration judge by a legal team that included Miller-Muro, and from all indications, it looked as if Kassindja's request for asylum would be denied and she would be sent back to Africa.

The outcome changed, both quickly and for the better, after her case caught the attention of *New York Times* reporter Celia Dugger. Dugger wrote a lengthy story not only about Kassindja's cry for help, but also exposed the abusive practice of female genital mutilation. WOMAN'S PLEA PUTS TRIBAL RITUAL ON TRIAL was the story that dominated the front page of the *Times* and continued inside for two complete pages. It was huge and life changing for both Kassinda and Miller-Muro.

Publicists began calling Miller-Muro's home the morning the article appeared. Soon after, national media, including *ABC Nightline, Dateline NBC,* CNN and on and on, requested interviews. Steven Spielberg, Sally Field and Lauren Hutton all called to offer support. Hillary Clinton's office called too.

Most importantly, there was a call from the office of then-United States Attorney General Janet Reno, who suggested that Kassindja's legal team promptly file another request for parole on behalf of Kassindja, who was being detained in a prison pending outcome of her case.

Someone needed to sponsor Kassindja upon her release, and scrambling to meet a tight legal deadline, Miller-Muro turned to the leaders of her religion, the National Spiritual Assembly of the Bahá'ís of the United States. Sponsorship agreement was reached with a local Bahá'í community after a quick telephone conference call; the papers were filed with the court; and Kassindja soon experienced freedom in her new home country, the United States.

In order to justify the government's reversal of its position, Reno's office issued a press release citing "new developments" that had come to light in the case, as well as the sponsorship by the Bahá'í community.

Times reporter Dugger ended up writing nearly a half dozen stories about the Kassindja case, and each time, the tone and news angle of her story both stimulated coverage by other news organizations and influenced what other journalists reported.

"The media attention made it become an important case to the courts and government," Miller-Muro shared with me. A group of judges who heard the case almost unanimously granted Kassindja's request for asylum. There was only one dissenting opinion.

The staggering amount of media coverage from the Kassindja case led to a best-selling book titled *Do They Hear You When You Cry*, which was coauthored by Kassindja and Miller-Muro and published by Bantam Doubleday. Miller-Muro used her advance and all her proceeds from the book to launch the Tahirih Justice Center, which is located just outside Washington, D.C., in Falls Church, Va. The justice center is a legal advocate for a wide range of issues faced by immigrant and refugee women, and it is sometimes a woman's only nonpartisan force for true justice.

Miller-Muro told me that in the beginning, dealing with media interviews was trial by fire, and with no formal training, she relied on instinct. She drew upon public speaking skills that her father had taught her. Aside from that, she relied on her own common sense and focused on communicating the truth with clear messages about what was right for her client.

"I learned how the media worked by watching TV interviews and reading articles to judge what they were looking for and who seemed most effective," she told me. "I began a practice that continues today: preparing one page of one-sentence quotes to memorize —those things that reflect points I want to be sure to make during an interview."

Miller-Muro gave me an example of the justice center's advocacy work on the issue of mail-order brides. The international marriage broker industry has exploded due to the Internet, and while some decent marriages may come from it, the unfortunate fact is that is has enabled the institution of marriage to be used as a way for predatory abusers to find their next victims. The Tahirih Justice Center has become a national leader on this issue, and while advocating for changes in laws that address the abuse of women through the international marriage broker industry, it has engaged a successful media campaign.

Regarding mail-order brides, Miller-Muro said, "The harsh reality is that the international marriage broker industry allows the institution of marriage to be used by violent predatory abusers to find their next victims." Such a line is a strong quotable quote that nearly always ends up in a story and influences an audience's perception.

"The sentence draws upon our sensibilities about the sanctity of marriage," she said. "And it communicates the need for a law that prevents predators from looking abroad for their next victim."

The justice center's media strategy on this issue has resulted in wide bipartisan support, the passage of a landmark piece of legislation regulating the international marriage broker industry, the win of the first lawsuit in the United States against an international marriage broker, and the attention of *Newsweek,* the *Washington Post, NBC Nightly News, The O'Reilly Factor* on Fox News and *The Tyra Banks Show.*

In the intervening years since the Kassindja case, Miller-Muro's voice — and that of others at the center — has been heard as the nonpartisan force for true justice countless times in the media, speaking out in support of women's issues.

The justice center's emphasis is on focused messages or talking points for what they want to communicate to influence an outcome. At the justice center, an interview's objective often is to influence judges, lawyers, lawmakers, members of congress and academics regarding legislation or court cases.

"Our preparation as an organization," she shared with me, "is to make sure we are all on the same page with the same talking points. We draft a three- to five-page document of main points we would like to make, with supporting arguments and statistics. From that document, we distill our talking points into a one-pager of five to ten sentences to deliver in an interview."

The justice center sends out periodic news releases on issues or developments, like a court decision or new legislation, but never expects a press release to result in a news story.

"Press releases are just a way to nudge a reporter to remind him or her that you are here and available to educate them on an issue," Miller-Muro said. "They see us as experts."

"We have never had success using press releases to generate media. It is just a way to keep them up-to-date on issues."

The justice center found the practice of blasting out press releases indiscriminately to countless reporters to be "completely ineffective," preferring instead to actively maintain a list of approximately 200 reporters who have expressed an interest in the organization or who write on their issues.

"I will call a few trusted reporters who have accurately reported on us to seek their advice on an issue or to share ideas," she said. "The truth is that the *New York Times*, the Associated Press and Reuters are the most powerful combination of media in the United States because their stories immediately appear in over 400 other newspapers, and TV media typically pick up stories from papers."

While Miller-Muro appreciates the power of television news to reach broad and general audiences, the impact does not last very long and does not always achieve the center's objectives. Print coverage, on the other hand, conveys greater credibility and lasts longer because it is archived by the large information databases, including LexisNexis.

When Miller-Muro or the justice center makes news, they find that print media is most powerful because people can cite it and quote it as an authority. Print media is far more influential in the field of human rights advocacy. Conversely, the general public has little direct influence on a court decision or piece of legislation.

To this day, the Tahirih Justice Center has never hired a public relations agency but prefers to work on a personal and pro bono level with a few communications consultants who believe in the work of the center and who willingly give their expertise for developing talking points or sharing media connections.

Long ago, Miller-Muro accepted responsibility for guiding the brand reputation of the Tahirih Justice Center and, in the process, developed a personal style to achieve consistent, meaningful coverage. You can benefit by following Miller-Muro's formula:

- Treat news releases only as a way to maintain awareness from reporters. Never expect a story to result from sending a release.

- Focus on a few journalists with whom you have a relationship — to pitch stories to or to ask for advice — avoiding mass outreach.

- Give reporters timely and relevant legitimate story angles, with personal stories that illustrate your point.

- Craft a page of five to 10 sentences — talking points or messages — that you want to say in an interview before ever speaking with a reporter.

- Develop healthy and respectful working relationships with journalists, which means being immediately responsive to their calls, respectful of their deadlines and corresponding in a professional manner.

- Readily admit when you are not an expert on an issue and refer journalists to other sources who are.

- Before speaking to reporters, look up their past coverage and understand their likely biases.

- Ask the journalist to use the name of your organization when quoting you so that your comments are best put into context.

Miller-Muro and her staff always personally handle the responsibility for developing and guiding the center's media strategy. That level of ownership and accountability is clearly one reason for the organization's enduring record of achieving important and sometimes life-changing media coverage, and it has put Layli Miller-Muro into that exclusive group of leaders who are among the world's most important communicators. Following her method can help you become a world-class communicator as well.

PART 3
Reaching. Engaging. Influencing.

Chapter Sixteen:
A Good Story Has Great Legs

Storytelling is perhaps the oldest form of effective communications ... and one of the timeliest. Today the use of storytelling cuts through competitive clutter far more effectively than anything else in an organization's marketing or PR arsenal, and it gets to the heart of what's special about your organization and what you have to say.

My colleague Anne Bell at PBS *NewsHour* says it best: "A great story has legs that in today's world can travel many miles per hour."

Anyone can do a PowerPoint presentation, write a dull report or press release or make detailed to-do lists for a stiffly structured meeting. Storytelling, on the other hand, conveys personality that everyone can identify with, and it can lead to transformational leadership that energizes all levels and corners of an organization.

The discipline of storytelling can energize (or reenergize) any business or organization. It becomes woven into the fabric, stimulates excitement and understanding of vision, builds consensus of purpose and triggers sharing, far and wide. In today's online world, the influence and payoff of good corporate storytelling can be staggeringly powerful.

As I have already written, one legendary example is Steve Jobs of Apple, regarded as one of today's best corporate storytellers and a master at capturing the media's attention.

Jobs' greatest strength is his personal certainty in his beliefs. He is inspiring and passionate about what he has to say. When he speaks of an Apple product, for example, you begin to believe that it is the greatest device ever created because Steve Jobs believes it is so. His transparency is an astonishingly powerful strength in communication and as a leader in today's online world.

What Jobs says is meaningful, and his broad audiences repeat it over and over because we believe that he speaks from his heart. Jobs is unquestionably one of the most charismatic business leaders on the planet, which brings up the logical question of whether charisma is a gift or if it is learned.

Based on my years of advising and working closely with top leaders of business in handling communications issues, I agree with Tom Stewart, chief marketing and knowledge officer of the global management consulting company Booz & Company, who says that mastery of charisma is achieved through hard work and deliberate practice. Anyone can become charismatic; it just takes a lot of work and expert coaching.

People who learn the skill of charisma develop a special level of self-awareness and self-knowledge, and they know how to communicate and connect with audiences through life stories that forge powerful communities, both in and outside their organizations. They speak from the heart. How they communicate vision and ideas becomes emblematic of what their organization is.

Conversely, as Stewart maintains, noncharismatic executives can barely fill the space around their shoes.

When it comes to enhancing an organization's reputation, storytelling can have distinctive benefits. Audiences will understand an organization's purpose more easily and clearly because sharing ideas, information and news through stories is a natural style of communications.

In today's digital environment, there is no debate over whether a company needs to choose between using online social media or face-to-face communications. It's not an either/or situation. It has to be both.

Consider the power of storytelling in your own organization as an approach to get everyone on the same page, pointed in the same direction, and energized with a story to share ... with someone else. One great story smoothly cuts across all boundaries to influentially achieve a common purpose in an organization's daily conversations:

- Shareholder/financial communications
- Internal communications
- Web sites, blogs, social media

- Media relations and external relations
- Government and regulator relations
- New business development

The list could go on, but you get the point. With storytelling, you are building enthusiasm at all levels within an organization, and outwardly to everyone touched by your organization. It is because people like to share good news. The walls of political silos crumble beneath the inspiration, passion and appeal of a good story.

One big benefit that will deliver immediate value and distinction to any business organization is that storytelling helps an organization get out of the old inward-looking and bad habit of talking about itself. It's like corporate navel gazing.

Here is the truth, even though it's a bitter pill to accept: No one cares about you. When I say that during lectures or consulting, it always gets attention, and I get glares of either anger or puzzlement. But it's a fact that no one cares about you or your organization. What people care about is how they benefit from your organization's services or products. How will their lives be enriched, made easier? That's what they care about — they care about themselves.

All the boring boilerplate in your press releases and all those glowing words of self-promotion on your Web site are a waste of time. No one cares. But give people a terrific story to share, and that's a different matter.

People like to share good news, so give them a story that they will get excited about and share with someone else. Increased media coverage, enhanced word of mouth and greater awareness all build exponentially from a great story that is carried by many legs.

What does a great story look like? As someone who began his career in network television news and then moved to a second career in public relations, storytelling is second nature, as it is for many of us.

Storytelling is about life. It is about sharing the human experience, something that is a common thread that tends to touch and connect with something inside each of us that makes us laugh, or perhaps cry, or maybe just contemplate. When we hear a story that touches a deep place in our hearts or life experience, we have a natural tendency to share it with someone else. We listen to a great story, and we often will retell it to a family member, friend or colleague. And so the story begins to breathe and take life.

As I find often during consulting, storytelling can easily be used to communicate vision, concepts, ideas and build consensus for an organization or company. Organizational storytelling highlights what's special and helps to achieve sustained image and reputation leadership.

If you are the storyteller, you must love your story. You must believe in what you are sharing, passionately. You must bring it to life so that the story is right there, living between you and the audience.

There are as many different kinds of stories as colors in the rainbow. That rainbow comes alive every autumn at the National Storytelling Festival in Jonesborough, Tenn. If you are interested in learning the spectrum of storytelling that might be applied to your organization, that's the place to hear amazing storytellers and learn techniques. But here's the common thread: Each story is about people and the experiences of people. The stories aren't about concrete roads, buildings, companies, software, products or manufacturing plants; they're about people, most often an individual who has experienced something in life. The story could even be about the storyteller.

The late Michael Deaver, my old friend and colleague, was a masterful storyteller. He said that good storytelling must contain emotional, logical and analytical elements, working together to capture attention. I agree. The emotional piece touches our hearts; the logical piece just makes sense; and the analytical part is supported by facts and figures. We can tell a great story that might lack either the logical or analytical pieces, but it has to connect with the audience emotionally in order to really work.

Storytelling must also be timely and relevant to what's happening in the world around us. Otherwise, while it could be a good story, it would lack perspective and context. Storytelling has a beginning as simple as *Let me tell you a story*, a middle that contains an event or experience, and an ending that wraps up the story with, perhaps, a lesson learned or a surprise twist.

I find it odd that while many people in communications agree about the value of organizational storytelling, few practice it. We tend to get hung up on using tactics, like the merits of using Twitter and Facebook or creating a corporate blog. But such tactics by themselves do not lead to inspiring communications or leadership for an organization ... without a story. There's got to be a significant paradigm shift in the advertising, marketing and public relations trades — from being overly obsessed with marketing, sales and promotion to embracing a new style that is more sharing, more inclusive, more conversational, more open, more credible and transparent.

Brooke Gladstone of National Public Radio's "On the Media" program says, "Journalists are taught to talk and write in human terms. Tell me a story."

We are all part of a storytelling culture in America. It's been that way forever, and it's no different in countries, cultures and communities around the world. We share an infinite variety of stories about the human experience, and often the best stories are repeated over and over.

Stories are the bedrock of interaction, building blocks of knowledge, the foundation of memory and learning. Stories connect us with our humanness and link past, present and future by teaching us to anticipate the possible consequences of our actions. Stories help define what is authentically special about something or someone.

Yet the power of storytelling is too often overlooked or dismissed as companies, nonprofits, associations and other organizations strive to get attention. They embrace, instead, a copycat style of communications — press releases, statements, promotions, marketing tactics and run-of-the-mill advertising — in an attempt to promote, market, sell or push publicity. And it does not work, especially in today's online world. It simply is no longer effective.

We are not living in a time when shouting, promoting, selling and pushing publicity works as it might have in the past.

Let me share an example of storytelling that favorably impacted the lives of some young people. High school students in Pomona, Calif., a town hard-hit by the 2009 economic downturn, worked with their teacher to create a video called "Is Anyone Listening?" In it, they shared stories of how each of their lives was impacted by home foreclosures, layoffs and economic hard times. They told of how their families were suffering and how they were going hungry.

They put the video on YouTube, and a local newspaper picked up the story. Then reporter John Larson of KCET Television, the PBS station in Los Angeles, reported the story. His piece was a magnificent example of journalistic storytelling. Next, the national PBS news program *NewsHour with Jim Lehrer* aired Larson's story. President Obama heard about the plight of the students and personally visited with them during a trip to California, pledging that he, the president of the United States, was listening to them.

The students in Pomona captured enormous worldwide attention by sharing their story, and they sure got attention for it.

How can this apply to you? Any company or organization, even if a small business or individual consultant, has a distinctive story. Find it by listening. Share it. Discuss it. Build upon it. Get others to repeat your story over and over.

Remember, storytelling has been the bedrock of interactive communications for at least a gazillion years before the Internet came along. Things like blogs, Twitter, Facebook, MySpace[38] and the sort are merely delivery methods or tactics. Strategic communications leadership begins with learning the craft of storytelling, an art form with many legs.

---

[38] www.myspace.com

Chapter Seventeen:
Perception Is Just Reality's Mirror Image

Perception is an influential, invisible and powerful force in communications. We make decisions based on how we perceive something or someone. And no two perceptions are exactly alike. People can be poles apart in their perception of something and both be "right" because their perceptions define their reality.

During our individual life journeys, we each have endless learning experiences and challenges that influence our perceptions. Suppose you and I see a cloud. It reminds you of the Wyeth painting of a giant with a club; to me, it looks like rain coming. Two different perceptions, both correct up to a point and certainly our own truths.

The dictionary defines *perception* as "intuitive recognition of a truth." In fact, perception is far more complex, intangible and fragile than that.

When jockeying to capture audience awareness, too many companies try to be what they hope to be, whether it's accurate or not. They seek a basic truth or reality in hopes it will set their organization apart from others: we're the *leading* … or the *largest* …

Unfortunately, this strategy lumps them into an enormous universe of other organizations saying the same thing. It's a boast that won't cut through competitive clutter. The public and the media are increasingly well informed. We've grown cautious of big claims and alert to and suspicious of the overuse of superlatives, especially when the declarations are not backed up by a compelling track record. The overuse of self-aggrandizing adjectives used to be a popular style, especially among technology companies during the tech boom of the late 90s yet today it often demotes potential for authentic credibility.

The conscious and subconscious factors that influence perception have been debated for centuries by academics, philosophers and, more recently, by the less-skilled perspective of communications professionals. And still your perception of something tomorrow might be different than it is today and may have changed today from what it was yesterday. That's human nature and the nature of perceptions. We perceive events, people, companies, products and things in different ways, and we are all motivated by our individual perceptions.

Not surprisingly, understanding perception is critically important in practicing communications today. We want to, of course, strive for accuracy and clarity in what we tell the media, thus reducing chances for confusion and misperceptions. We may both be right when we see different things in the cloud; but in strategic communications, the perception that counts is often that of the media.

Here's an example: If you have a policy that anything said to the media must be cleared in advance by an attorney, then you could be building a perception with reporters of being defensive and that you have something to hide.

The same is true if you read from a prepared statement in response to routine questions from reporters or make the media jump through hoops as they try to get information on your Web site. Whether or not you read accurately, you are sending a signal of defensiveness. If your organization is already in hot water, you don't want to exacerbate the situation by acting evasive.

Here are six steps that I counsel companies, individuals and organizations to take to enhance and manage a perception:

- *Get outside yourself.* Look at your image challenge from the perspective of an outsider, such as a client or customer or investor or the media. Understand how others see you.

- *Walk into the future.* Define how you want your organization to be described two or three years from now by people who are important to your company.

- *Challenge conventional thinking.* Just because something felt good a couple of years ago doesn't mean it will work in today's highly competitive arenas. It's okay — in fact, necessary

— to discard bad habits in communications and try new approaches.

- *Avoid "committee speak."* Defining your organization by committee often results in too many words that say too little, too vaguely.

- *Steer away from overused 50-cent marketing words.* You know what they are: the dull adjectives pulled off the shelf when we can't think of anything else. Words like *unique, innovative* and *leading provider* have been overworked to the point of becoming meaningless.

- *Be consistent.* Once you have decided what to say and how to say it, stick with that consistent approach in working with the news media. Consistency builds trust and helps overcome confusion that can adversely influence an otherwise good perception.

In striving for communications leadership, it doesn't matter whether you are the "largest" or the "best." If your organization is perceived as one that communicates openly, candidly and clearly, then you are sending positive signals to your audiences, including the news media. It helps others perceive you as a winner.

Chapter Eighteen:
Plain Language Is Sexy

Plain language. It is clear, to the point and meaningful. Moreover, it's such a cool and different approach in many organizations that it has become sexy. Sexy because plain language is so appealing and attention getting.

In today's noisy world, where everyone seems to be shouting to get attention, there's no better way to cut through competitive clutter than with the instant clarity of plain language, which everyone understands because it's free of jargon, cliques and gobbledygook.

As a consultant, my astonishment never ceases to see how businesses and organizations develop their own internal languages that not everyone comprehends, including the people who work there. Presentations, for example, are often filled with enough overused hype and acronyms to make anyone's eyes glaze over.

HubSpot,[39] an Internet marketing company based in Cambridge, Mass., has developed an array of online evaluation tools, including a clever and free online device called the Gobbledygook Grader. Teaming up with thought leadership and marketing author David Meerman Scott and Dow Jones, they analyzed the most overused gobbledygook words in nearly three-quarters of a million press releases, sent in North American in 2008, to create the Gobbledygook Grader.[40]

The top overused and gobbledygook words included:

---

[39] www.hubspot.com
[40] http://gobbledygook.grader.com

- Innovative
- Unique
- Pleased/proud to
- Focused on
- Leading provider
- Commitment
- Partnership
- New and improved
- Leverage
- 120 percent
- Cost-effective
- Next generation
- World class
- High performance
- Value added

The Gobbledygook Grader effectively drives home the point that far too many — in fact, *most* press releases — are full of meaningless gobbledygook, jargon, and overworked hype-laden junk words.

This may be sobering news for people who write press releases or for organizations under the illusion that press releases will magically translate into media attention. But looking closer, I wonder whether the Grader is more of a simple tactic that does not address the real issue, the real problem.

Aside from the fact that now we have yet another online grader tool, there is really nothing new about the fact that press releases are generally not focused on providing legitimate news but instead are infused with meaningless promotional hype that few people care about. Today's press releases are less about giving the media something to report … and more about promoting something.

Many of today's press releases have become little more than sales flyers. That's why most news organizations use special spam filters, like SpamSieve,[41] which use clever algorithms to recognize and catch hype and remove press releases to e-mail trash.

Even though PR people and organizations crank out hundreds of thousands of releases, the reality is that the media sees few of them.

On the other hand, if, God forbid, an organization's intention is to generate a real news story, here's how:

---

[41] http://c-command.com/spamsieve

1. Write a brief story synopsis in plain language (free of all jargon, gobbledygook and junk words), no more than about 100 words.

2. Include the synopsis in an e-mail to a reporter who typically will write about such subjects.

3. Avoid using those expensive press release distribution services, such as Vocus, that blast material indiscriminately to thousands of reporters and bloggers, living and dead. People in the media are paid to find fresh, new stories, not to recycle what a competitor has written about.

4. Give the reporter or blogger a call a day later, not to ask whether he or she received your e-mail (because the person surely did), but rather to underscore the possible timeliness of your story suggestion and to offer to be a helpful resource.

Given today's seismic shakeout in the mainstream news industry, there is no magic formula for landing a news story, but the preceding four steps are about as close as you can get to one.

Plain language is the key because it stands out amongst all the noise, hype and clutter in today's competitive world.

For more than five decades, the late Lilyan Wilder was considered the foremost teacher and speech coach in America and guided the careers of countless celebrities, executives and politicians — including Oprah, Larry King, Maria Shriver, Charlie Rose, Binyamin Netanyahu, George H. W. Bush, Tom Brokaw and Charles Osgood.

Regardless of whom she was coaching, she insisted on the use of plain language and viewed junk words as those meaningless or ambiguous words that creep into everyday usage of English, causing confusion and derailing understanding. Ms. Wilder was emphatic that junk words must be avoided in order for any person to reach his or her full potential as an outstanding communicator.

In the practice of communications, we sometimes get lazy and use the jargon of an industry because it seems more precise, clearer and impressive than plain language. Too bad, because it is a trap where we forfeit any chance of gaining an edge and winning. We lose any chance at competitive differentiation and leadership.

Here's an easy five-step checklist to help you authentically trumpet the true value of your enterprise, using plain language, and separate the leaders from the losers:

- *Think and talk outside of yourself.* Most of the time, the news media and your primary audiences prefer to hear about the value of what your organization does, rather than adjective-filled pronouncements about your company. Invest the time in some high-level strategic thinking to define how you want your company to be perceived and talked about in two or three years. That strategy will help guide a positive brand-building marketing communications approach today and into the future.

- *Make strategic vision come alive.* To credibly and realistically achieve what's called *competitive positioning*, develop an original, practical and working strategic plan that uses clever tactics to gain attention. Remember, it doesn't really matter whether you are the "largest" or "best" organization. If you are viewed as a leader, you've won.

- *Stand in the shoes of your audiences.* Learn how to communicate the benefit of your product or service to the person who ultimately makes the decision and has the authority to buy.

- *Talk in sound bites, not elevator speeches.* A sound bite communicates your message or describes your endeavor, precisely, in one breath — about 16 seconds — while using words that are understandable, credible, exciting and memorable. An *elevator speech*, although popular, takes too long, particularly if you are headed up to the 44th floor. Reporters, distracted by others who can get to the point more concisely, will lose interest.

- *Avoid junk words — jargon, acronyms, buzzwords and trendy clichés.* Few phrases lead to more communication confusion and misunderstandings than the prefabricated and empty clichés of business and management consultants, such as *value proposition, actionable, learning partners, ramp up, empowering, maximizing, critical path* and *visioning*. This long list of ambiguous junk words probably originated in some business school years ago. With today's preference for transparency and plain language, avoid junk words. They can impede clear communication.

When used properly, these principles of effective communications deliver valuable results for any organization. Strategic communications require clear and precise differentiation so that the media and audiences know you from your competitor.

The challenge is to overcome a common thread among most companies: the inability to incisively and concisely describe their individual value and what's genuinely special about what they deliver to their audiences, their customers. Too often, the company stalls in its own words and obtuse, overworked business-school jargon.

Chapter Nineteen:
Die, Press Releases!

A friend was telling me about a conference she had just attended in Washington. It brought together a large group of public relations people with a smaller group of working journalists. The discussion had centered, as it often does at such sessions, on what journalists really need in today's demanding media world … as well as the merits of press releases.

The journalists unanimously had said that news releases are useless. In fact, news releases—which are shared with everyone under the sun through blast e-mail services — are the antithesis of what the media wants. Reporters, whether mainstream or online, are paid to find and report fresh and imaginative stories — stories that haven't appeared elsewhere. They cannot hope to keep their jobs by recycling promotional materials disguised as press releases.

The group of journalists told the PR people that all they really need is a brief, concisely written e-mail that outlines a story, and no follow-up phone calls to check whether they got the e-mail. The follow-up phone call generally reveals an insecure PR rookie. What the media does not need is for PR people to pursue them aggressively with press releases that rarely contain any elements of stories. Just give reporters a story idea and let them run with it. That's their job.

I know that most news releases today have morphed into something that's not really intended for the media but is instead self-serving promotion for an organization, glowing announcements of generally trivial nature to make the suits in the corner offices happy. But the morphing has polluted the media waters, and here's why: Many PR agencies today are shoveling out news releases to the media by the tens of thousands in a style that has not changed much for decades, except that today's digital delivery methods have replaced envelopes, stamps and fax machines. It no longer works.

Perhaps one of the most common "sins" of leaders and communications people is never actually identifying how to bridge the gap between what is *newsworthy* for the media and the promotional message they push on behalf of a client or employer.

Consequently, too many, if not most, media campaigns are centered around — maybe it's more accurate to say *hidden behind* — a systematic flood of news releases and expensive media materials that are sent out carpet-bomb style to the media, most often to the wrong people.

Out of fairness, many organizations have been sending out press releases for so long that it has become part of the corporate culture, regardless of whether it is effective. Public relations people are aware of old habits but rarely suggest more contemporary techniques for generating earned media coverage because helping a client distribute a press release is simple work for a junior staffer. It is easy, billable time.

It happens hundreds of times each day: An organization issues a news release via a paid news release wire service, such as PR Newswire, Vocus or BusinessWire, or through a service that bulk e-mails thousands of news contacts. Those e-mails are often caught in spam filters and never seen. Somehow, there is a feeling that if the news industry is smothered by a release, someone might pay attention.

On the contrary, such mass distribution is an unproductive way of getting the attention of today's news media, and it is about as effective as dropping thousands of copies of the release from an airplane, except that the latter might actually get some news coverage, although not very positive, I suspect.

Out of fairness, mass distribution of financial news announcements — for example, earnings reports and news of market and shareholder interest — provides an efficient way to meet disclosure requirements for publicly traded companies.

If you hope that a news release will somehow become a meaningful news story, whether in a newspaper, blog, TV newscast or anywhere else, I must respectfully inform you that you are mistaken. If you pay a press release distribution service to send your release to the news universe, you are taking the wrong approach and wasting money.

Journalists are paid to find fresh new stories that competitors don't have. Mass distribution means everyone has the same information. *USA Today* is typical of today's mainstream media. If you send them a news release that you have sent to everyone else or pitch a story that you have pitched to other news organizations, they will not touch it, regardless of how great it might sound. Why should they pay any attention to your news release that you have shared with the world?

Nonetheless, the paid news distribution services are also clogged with other poorly focused and irrelevant news releases that journalists tend to ignore many, if not most, of the releases because they just do not have the time to sort through all of them.

If there is one common trait among many people who are charged with working with the media, it is a reluctance to actually interface personally with the news media in any way, such as through a phone call. Odd as it might seem, too many public relations people hide behind news releases, media lists, mailings, bulk e-mails and faxes. They avoid actually picking up the phone to speak with a journalist to develop a working relationship.

Organizations spend fortunes on so-called news-distribution services to get their news releases and media materials in front of as many journalists as possible, seemingly to help them avoid having to go to the trouble of picking up a phone and making a personal pitch to a reporter.

It's fairly common to hear PR agency executives tell clients that an "exclusive" news service was used to get their release before several thousand reporters, as if to suggest that the PR people have vast contacts. Such claims can only be labeled as "murky truth."

The truth is that paid newswire services are frequently used to indiscriminately bombard the media with press releases, especially when PR people lack the right media contacts. It is an outdated and ineffective tactic at best. While a news distribution service might have the capability to send a news release to thousands of journalists via e-mail, there's no guarantee that anyone will actually really read it or even consider doing a story.

Today an increasing number of more savvy executives and strategic communications professionals are turning to newer and alternative approaches to produce meaningful results. These new approaches do not require sending out hundreds of news releases.

The process begins by crafting a legitimate news story, then focusing on only that handful of journalists who cover an organization. The technique is to build trusted relationships with journalists provide incisive information and set the stage to work with those journalists to develop a relevant and timely news story. That's the way to maximize control of your story and improve the chance that it will come out the way you hope.

How do you figure out what the media wants and needs? Simple: Pretend you are a reporter and that your only stake in the matter is in getting a good story, not in getting your message out. In other words, put yourself in the reporter's shoes and offer what he or she is looking for. Get his or her attention and then work on developing a meaningful message or story.

Protecting an organization's reputation is ultimately the responsibility of the executive at the top, aided by competent communications people, so isn't it time to roll up your sleeves and master all the strategies, tactics, tools and nuances?

- Get to know journalists and bloggers who cover your business or organization on a first-name basis. Chances are there are just a few.

- Pick up the telephone and have a conversation.

- Find out what information they need, how they want it and when.

- Build trust and an open exchange of ideas.

- Establish yourself as a regular resource of tips and information, which gives you an opportunity to stay in contact with the journalists and bloggers.

- Develop the skill of communicating your organization's vision and news through an engaging form of storytelling.

Then, whether you have legitimate news or need to manage a crisis, pick up the phone and talk with the right person in the media. That's how the best stories happen. That's how to best manage your messages, and what the media, both online and mainstream, says about you.

Communicating to today's media is not blitzing everyone in the newsroom with the same news release or media kit. It all comes down to establishing a trusted relationship, making phone calls to news organizations, identifying the right journalists and presenting an interesting, timely and relevant story in the brief and incisive manner that reporters prefer.

Chapter Twenty:
Nothing Is Secret, or "No Comment"

In today's world of e-mail, the Internet and instant messaging, it's folly to think that anything is secret. Documents, notes from meetings, photos, anything — regardless of the level of confidentiality — can be sent across town or around the world or show up on a blog in a flash with a single click of a mouse. It happens all the time. Someone thought he could keep photos of detainee torture and abuse at Baghdad's Abu Ghraib prison secret, and we all know what happened. Politicians try to hide paramours, but someone will almost always tip off the media.

What's more, there has been a proliferation of blogs devoted to finding out and revealing secrets about companies and organizations. MacRumors,[42] for example, trades gossip, rumors and facts about Apple, the notoriously secretive computer company. Apple inspires considerable speculation among consumers, Wall Street and in the technology industry because of its penchant — some call it obsession — for secrecy.

MacRumors has attracted such a large number of fans that it has been listed among the "25 most valuable blogs" on the Internet, and it has become a moneymaking venture for the site's founder, Dr. Arnold Kim. In fact, MacRumors is turning a nice profit through income from banner ads, commissions on product sales and Google advertising, allowing Dr. Kim to leave his full-time job in medicine to earn a six-figure income as full-time blogger and work from home.

Success stories about popular and profitable blogs, like MacRumors, have spawned similar sites that focus on other organizations. Apple is not the only company trying to keep secrets.

---

[42] www.macrumors.com

In strategic communications, the moment you sit down to write any document, whether a news release or strategic plan or e-mail, you must keep in mind that whatever you draft could become public, even inadvertently. Nothing is secret.

Throughout this book, I have stressed the importance of truthfulness and transparency in getting your story out and working with the news media. As I wrote earlier, communications with the news media mirrors behavior. An organization that dodges facts and manipulates issues will ultimately erode whatever credibility it may have. What happened at the Washington, D.C., zoo a few years ago is a classic example.

Under Dr. Lucy Spelman's watch as director of the National Zoo in Washington, nearly two dozen animals died, including some rare and endangered species. Some veterinary records were changed after the fact. In one case, a popular elephant died of tuberculosis at an early age because of lack of an easily obtainable vaccination. In another case, two rare zebras died from hypothermia and malnutrition. It all came to light through a series of reports in the *Washington Post*.

How did the *Post* know? Somebody talked. A front-page story by Henri E. Cauvin had all the grisly details: "In a confidential strategy paper produced by (PR agency) Hill & Knowlton, the zoo is urged to be open with the media but aggressive in containing any fallout from the deaths." The leaked 23-page confidential plan warns that continuing inquiries by the *Washington Post* could make it emerge as a story of national import, creating a crisis that would imperil the zoo's bid for full accreditation and threaten the job of Director Lucy H. Spelman.

"Lucy Spelman's credibility as a leader may appear to be diminished, with possible requests for her removal," Hill & Knowlton said in a list of potential scenarios that could follow more negative news stories about her role at the zoo.

The result was that Spelman paid the PR firm $50,000 of the zoo's money to try to clean up her image, but it backfired. Her scheme became front-page news. It created a perception that good PR for her was more important than taking responsible and affirmative steps to ensure the safe welfare of zoo animals. Zoo employees were outraged by her behavior, and confidential documents got into the hands of a reporter. The resulting series of stories portrayed Spelman as an inept zoo director and Hill & Knowlton as more concerned about her reputation and a nice fee than that of the zoo.

It didn't stop there. The arrogance of the zoo's leader resulted in a *Washington Post* editorial that began this way: "If only the animals could talk, we might learn more troubling truths about their care and feeding at the National Zoo. Incomplete or altered veterinary records have obscured instances of apparent neglect, misdiagnosis and other serious mistakes in connection with the deaths of at least 23 animals ..."

News is leaked to the media every day when unusual things happen. Nothing, absolutely nothing, can be kept secret. The more egregious the sin, the more likely it will make it to the media. Remember the infamous Deep Throat of Nixon's Watergate, the Pentagon papers that the courageous Daniel Ellsberg released to the *New York Times*, which exposed the cover-ups? That was decades ago, long before e-mail, blogs, the Internet and a 24-hour news cycle. Secrecy is much harder, if not impossible, to pull off today.

Apple takes secrets seriously, as I have mentioned. Secrecy is just not part of the communications strategy; it is baked into the corporate culture. If an employee discusses a new product under development with anyone but a team member, the result is instant termination. It's all clearly spelled out for the company's employees, who are required to sign confidentiality agreements.

At Apple, there is no leniency for employees who talk out of school. Tell a secret, and it's termination. Not surprisingly, Apple is noted for controlling the flow of news and announcements to the greatest benefit to the company.

Although you can't expect anything to be secret forever, you can maximize your chances of confidentiality and minimize your chances of damaging your reputation. Here are some tips on handling information before it goes public:

- *Label a draft as a draft.* When writing a document, such as a news release and media-briefing document, type DRAFT at the top of the first page. Include draft version number, date and your own initials. Then, if the document becomes public prematurely, your organization has a legitimate defense that the document was a draft, not a final statement.

- *Avoid e-mailing everyone.* It's a bad habit at many organizations to include extraneous people on e-mails. Limit e-mail daisy chains. Especially on issues of your organization's image and reputation, only share e-mails and documents between people who are relevant to the topic.

- *Have signed confidentiality statements.* Employees will often think twice before leaking sensitive material when they've signed a confidentiality statement that clearly spells out that termination may result from intentionally telling secrets.

Of course, the best chance you might have at handling leaks is the time you invest in developing personal relationships with the reporters and bloggers who cover your organization. You can develop credibility with the media that will no doubt eclipse that of a sometimes-anonymous informant.

There's nothing better in a potentially hostile media environment than to be on a first-name basis with key members of the media. Having an established and trusted professional relationship can work to turn around wrong impressions, correct misinformation, help defuse a possibly unfavorable story, and provide a better and more accurate perspective for journalists.

If you are facing tough issues that the media will ask you about, and you want to shout "No comment!" you might as well hold up a big red sign that reads *Guilty!* The end result will be about the same. It is simply irresponsible for a spokesperson to say "No comment," for it will usually result in more damage. Veteran business reporter Luladey Tadesse told me that "no comment" is really a comment. "It makes you look defensive," she said. She is so correct.

To a professional journalist, "No comment" can be a telltale sign of a bigger problem.

During 30 years as a journalist and strategic communications consultant, I can't tell you the number of times I've seen bad situations worsen because a spokesperson decided to say, usually in a curt tone of voice, "No comment" to the media, rather than find a better response.

Not only does saying "No comment" reflect a lack of professional communications expertise, but those two words can inflict lasting damage on an organization's brand and reputation.

"No comment" immediately creates a feeling of fear and mistrust about an individual or organization, regardless of the circumstances. It suggests guilt, arrogance and abruptness — all the emotional elements you want to avoid during a supercharged situation. It implies that you have something to hide. Whatever the level of desperation, frustration and aggravation when things go badly, those two words are never an option. Never.

It usually happens because some attorney mandates that the company say nothing but "No comment." That is irresponsible and shows disregard for an organization's image and reputation. Attorneys may know the law, but few of them know or comprehend the changing methods and elements for effective communications in the digital era. If an organization puts an attorney in charge of communications, problems may result.

Here is an alternative approach to handling a potentially damaging situation for your organization or yourself:

First, when a reporter calls you, remember that there is no law that says you must talk with the reporter at that moment. If you feel unprepared or ambushed, buy some time to collect your thoughts and think of something to say. Explain to the reporter that you are more than happy to speak with him or her, but you are in the middle of something. Ask if he or she is on deadline and negotiate a reasonable time frame during which to return the call, such as a half hour to one hour later.

Second, and this is essential, ask the reporter to give you an idea of what he or she wants to talk about. Never ask reporters what questions they are going to ask; just query the subject matter. Most reporters will work with you. Then get together with your communications people and others to formulate a meaningful statement other than "No comment." Buying some time is an invaluable tool in strategic communications because it allows you to get over being nervous about talking with a reporter, possibly over an adverse issue, and helps you to focus. Finally, and this too is really important, contact the reporter as promised.

If your organization is facing an unfavorable situation that might draw media questions, it is essential to work in advance of any media contact and develop a response or statement, no matter how brief it might be. Think of it as a good opportunity to turn around a negative perception. A possible response could begin something like this: "While we are not prepared to make a formal statement at this time …" and then bridge one or two brief, important messages about the situation. In that way, you give the impression of being responsive, responsible and accountable.

A bridge is an interview tactic to control and redirect an interview back to the subject that you want to talk about, using the salient messages that you have developed and rehearsed in advance.

Third, remember that it's okay to be brief. In fact, the fewer words, the better, as long as they are not "No comment." The media will accept a response that's only a sentence or two because at least you are taking the time to say *something* during a difficult time.

Show genuine sincerity and a willingness to communicate … whether you feel it or not. A positive attitude often will communicate as much as actual words will. It may be your only constructive option.

If faced with a developing possibly negative situation, consider saying this: "We want to be clear and accurate in anything we say. We are still gathering information that we will share with you when we have the whole picture."

In other words, there are many statements you can make to the news media other than "No comment." View an adverse situation as an opportunity to briefly deliver positive messages that communicate responsiveness and concern.

Chapter Twenty-One:
Strategic Planning While You Wait

More than ever, I am convinced we live in a tactics-driven world, and it's leading us in a downward direction. When we embrace tactics, we relinquish leadership, by default. Using tactics reveals a level of anxiety over needing to get results fast, at any price, and often with not much depth of quality or meaning. Good results don't work that way, especially in today's online digital environment.

In business and everyday living, we are awash in top 10 steps to solve this or that. Top 10 things to make money, top 10 things to get attention, top 10 ways to look more beautiful, top 10 things to be recognized as a winner, and so on. While they might be fun to read, these are all just tactics and most often lack strategic substance and purpose. Many PR people, however, love tactics because they require little thought, seem easy and are checklists of things to do that make us think we've accomplished something. This is just an illusion.

Tactics without carefully thought-out strategies almost certainly lead to unsatisfactory results, missteps or failure. Tactics lack inspiration, passion, cohesive purpose and focus. It's like walking in circles, getting nowhere meaningful.

Yet we are living in a culture where tactics are popular because they are easy. Strategic purpose, on the other hand, requires imaginative ideas, intelligent process, organization and work. Strategies deliver desired results, and strategic planning is not rocket science. And here's the best part: developing strategies is fast and quite easy.

However, the traditional approach to strategic planning has become too complicated, in my opinion. It's reached the point where developing a strategy, as espoused by many consultants, is simply too time-consuming, too divisive and too frustrating a process. It's dreaded at many organizations.

Years ago, I had a business partner, the late Jon Phelps, who, like me, always looked for practical solutions to assist clients with fast results. Most of all, we shared a dislike for the overly complicated style of strategic planning that's taught in many business schools, an approach that requires weeks, wastes valuable time, and results in a plan that people either hate or rarely understand because it is so wordy and complicated.

So, we created the SOS approach to strategic planning, a way to keep it clear, easy, straightforward and, most of all, actually fun. This method for developing a plan gets people excited and delivers meaningful results on time. Jon called it strategy planning while you wait.

SOS means Situation Objectives Strategies — the foundation of a strategic plan. Add to that the components of identifying audiences, developing messages that resonate favorably with those audiences, tactics that bring the strategies to life, a timeline, and a measurement matrix, and an SOS results in an action-packed business communications plan that can be developed in a few days, builds consensus and delivers.

The key is to use common sense, plain language and never become tangled up in silly things that don't matter, like whether something is a goal or an objective (because it's all the same).

The process of developing an organization's strategic communications cannot be delegated to staff members who may not be aware of the whole picture. Today's top executive leader needs to be involved, at least in defining the vision that he or she wants to communicate, as well as the primary positioning messages to precisely differentiate the organization from competitors.

Strategic communications planning is a process that need not be difficult or time-consuming.

Think of the elements of effective strategic communications as the three legs on a stool that allows you to stand above the crowd and be seen. Take away one or two legs, and you'll fall off. Add too many legs, and the stool becomes awkward and unmanageable. Here are the three pillars:

Pillar One: The Strategic Communications, or SOS Plan. A plan gives focus to your purpose and your objectives. Why would any organization ever consider launching an outreach program or making any public statement without some sort of plan that provides purpose, relevance and context?

Effective strategic communications begins with a carefully thought-out plan to position an organization competitively. The plan embraces the overall corporate vision and objectives, giving focus, purpose and reason to a communications effort. It does not begin with tactics or with copying tactics that you've seen other people use to boost visibility in the media. It begins with asking yourself candid and tough questions that will help you put your fingers on the distinct pulse of your organization and identify precisely the right ways and the best words to enhance your image before key audiences. Some of those questions are:

- What's so special about your organization that makes it stand out from anyone else, and who cares beyond the company parking lot? What are the things about your company that appeal most to the people who really matter outside, those who rely on your organization, such as customers, employees, investors, buyers, vendors and stakeholders?

- How do you want your company described by others — in clear, jargon-free words? In other words, how do you think your best customer might describe why you were chosen over a competitor?

- What is genuinely newsworthy about your organization's products or services? Keep in mind that no one cares about your company. Really. They only care about how your organization might benefit them.

Think of a strategic communications plan as a beacon that will guide important audiences to your organization. A strategic communications plan mirrors the objectives of a company's business plan and works to bring the strategic business plan to life more efficiently and more compellingly than any other method.

Most of all, it helps organizations get outside themselves, and into fresh, new conversations and interactions with their publics.

The SOS plan's components are straightforward:

- *Situation overview*: a few paragraphs to summarize the lay of the land, competitive environment, challenges and obstacles, as well as advantages and opportunities. This is your opportunity to say, "Here's what we're up against, here's what we're going to do and here's how we're going to make it happen."

- *Audiences*: a list of all audiences that you intend to reach through your media initiative — internal and external, public and highly specialized. I've always observed a natural tendency to create a list that's too long yet often omits the media, mainstream or online. Sometimes we even list an audience group that's no longer relevant to our business. Challenge yourself about who's important, and who is not. Here's your chance to fine-tune that list and reduce it to the essentials.

- *Positioning statement*: an introductory sentence or two that distinctly and clearly differentiates the value delivered by your organization from your competitors and works to capture the attention of your key audiences.

- *Objectives*: preferably three and certainly no more than four goals that reflect and complement the aim of your organization's business plan. Begin each objective with an active word, such as *boost* or *enhance* or *create*. You can also use the old style of beginning each objective with the word *to*.

- *Strategies*: having a specific strategy for achieving each objective. Describe in inspiring detail how you intend to achieve the objectives. In other words, how you plan to get from here to there. Remember that you cannot list an objective without a strategy for making it happen. Additionally, you can only have one strategy per objective in order to keep the SOS plan streamlined and effective.

- *Tactics*: unique and distinctive action points that will bring your strategies to life in order to achieve the objectives.

- *Measurement*: a mechanism to demonstrate tangible results. Elements can include an upward trend in such measurable points as sales, new business leads, stock value, media coverage, increased Web site traffic and unsolicited praise from people who are important to the organization. Create a *measurement matrix*, a chart that tracks each component and clearly shows achievements.

- *Timeline:* how the plan will be executed in a timely fashion, and when you can expect to start seeing results.

Be mindful of not allowing tactics to drive the planning process. *Tactics are the fun side of planning, while objectives and strategies require more thought.* Consequently, people too often jump to tactics that may or may not be relevant to the plan. That could lead to wasted time, wrong strategic directions and costly mistakes.

Tactics will, however, naturally be revealed in a communications plan developed using the SOS strategic planning process because they will be connected clearly with objectives and strategies. There will be no spinning of wheels, no false moves. SOS planning tactics will show what to do first: for example, how and whether to use the communications power of Web 2.0 or more traditional techniques.

Pillar Two: Be Original. While it always helps to know your competition, ignore what they are saying and how they are saying it. Although a competitor may do something cool, it may not be either smart or effective. If there's a news story about that company or organization and you're not mentioned, forget it. As with the city bus, another opportunity will soon come along before you know it. If you copy or react to the featured organization, you have, by default, put yourself in second place, making yourself a "wannabe" in the media's eyes. The media and the public do not gravitate to wannabes.

Ignore what the competition says to the media. Chart new territory. Be original and imaginative because you are smarter and savvier than they are. If you become passionate, inspiring and credible in communications, the competition won't matter because more people will pay attention to you. More importantly, as I have previously written, focus on what your customers or buyers really care about: the benefit and value that what your organization makes or sells brings to their lives. Again, never talk about your company or organization, because no one cares.

There's too much competitive clutter out there in the marketplace these days. You cannot afford to be ordinary. Throw out conventional wisdom and old-school, traditional approaches for working with the media. I've often said that conventional wisdom is a code phrase for dull and predictable.

Challenge the claims and promises of your public relations agency, if you have one. Forget news releases and expensive media kits. Don't fall into the trap of feeling compelled to announce every little event that happens at your place. Your organization has special things to say, so why say them in a predictable and boring fashion?

An essential part of being original is using clever visuals. If you want to quickly leapfrog your image and reputation out ahead of your competition, think about three things: visuals, visuals, visuals. Nothing captures the media's attention faster than great pictures.

When it comes to what makes it on the air, a TV news producer most often will go with a second-class story that has great visuals over a better story without visuals. That's just the way journalism works, and it's not going to change. Television news, online news outfits, blogs, newspapers and other media are mostly driven by visuals over content.

Pillar Three: Tell the Truth. Regardless of the situation and circumstances, accuracy, transparency and candor in dealing with the media is always the best route.

We have all learned in recent years of far too many examples and stories of deception and lies in communications and public statements: Wall Street's financial meltdown, torture of foreign prisoners by the United States, political misdeeds and corporate wrongdoing, just to name a few.

Today we are living in a new era, when nothing remains secret, and openness is paramount. In today's world of communicating through the media — when what you say can be heard around the world in a split second — imaginative ideas, transparency and the truth win out every day of the week over thread-worn conventional wisdom, such as manipulation, parsing words and hype.

Many of today's most highly visible and respected business leaders have invested the time to develop a plan for competitive image and reputation leadership through the use of credible communications. They have dared to step outside the box of what everyone else is doing and saying in order to build awareness with imaginative ideas and approaches. Most of all, they are earning our trust and respect by being open and transparent.

Chapter Twenty-Two:
Mission Statements Are Useless

If there is one issue that separates today's savvy leader from wannabes, it is recognizing the meaningless value of mission statements when what an organization really desires is better brand awareness.

Boosting awareness for a business, not-for-profit organization or association doesn't start or end with a mission statement. In fact, mission statements are a waste of time in today's world because they are singularly inward looking and useless, sort of like organizational navel gazing.

John Rock, an executive for more than three decades at the now-defunct Oldsmobile division of General Motors, described mission statements this way: "A bunch of guys take off their ties and coats, go into a motel room for three days, put a bunch of words on a piece of paper and then go back to business as usual."

Based on years as a journalist and in strategic communications, my opinion of mission statements is that most are trivial and fail to help inspire an organization, improve a brand or reputation or enhance competitive success.

If you read them closely, mission statements don't make a lot of sense. They are frequently a pastiche of irrelevant buzzwords designed to sound lofty, reassuring, authoritative and boring. The end result too often is a "Who cares?" effect.

Moreover, there is not a legitimate use or place for mission statements in the digital era. In the online environment, where sharp, clear and believable communications gain prominence, mission statements tend to sound old-fashioned and lack incisive distinction and importance. The words are too vague and one-size-fits-all.

Pamela Goett, who worked for the Journal of Business Strategy, dug into the origins of mission statements and wrote this reality check:

> *A handful of years ago, some guru opined that mission statements were absolutely critical to a company's success. So a lot of firms packed their most senior people off to expensive retreats to prepare this vital document. And the executives took the task very, very seriously (which is why so many mission statements sound so stuffy). The hoopla over mission statements and vision has a lot in common with the cheers for the emperor's new clothes. It's applause for delusions, for quick fixes for something that needs more thought and planning than can be expressed in a calligraphic paragraph.*

It has been said that organizations invest otherwise productive time to develop mission statements when they don't know who they are or why they are special.

During a lecture not long ago, before several hundred young and highly educated business professionals from 44 countries, who were meeting at the Townsend International School in the Czech Republic, I asked for a show of hands of people who had been involved in developing mission statements. Nearly every hand went up.

Then I asked for a show of hands from people who felt there was any value in mission statements. No hands went up. None.

Nevertheless, many organizations seem to have a curious need to waste time creating mission statements these days, and I suspect without ever asking why. There is just a current naïve belief that mission statements will magically transform an organization, leading to success or, at the very least, making the top managers look smart.

By contrast, I advise clients to focus quality time and real thought on positioning statements, where the words can create genuine and authentic competitive brand differentiation.

Why, you may ask, are positioning messages important when we seek to find more effective ways to communicate our messages and news to publics? Here is the answer: Because one of our primary goals is to communicate a subtle differentiating message about the true value of *our* organizations to audiences, including the media. Positioning statements help you to be remembered. We want an audience to form a good impression about the importance and quality of your organization's products and services.

What's the difference between a mission statement and a positioning message? There's a big difference. Here's a guide:

A mission statement tells people who are close to your organization where you hope to go in a perfect world. It is idealistic and filled with words that tell people you are nice and kind to small children and animals. But it is not the real world, merely a quest (hence the name *mission* statement).

It usually describes the future in terms of a search for growth or a promise of unparalleled integrity. Who can argue with that? Yet mission statements do not detail how to meet goals or state why a customer might hire your company or buy your products over a competitor's.

By definition, mission statements don't talk about where you are today or, more importantly, your competitive edge, but only mention what you hope to achieve. Mission statements, like too many advertising, promotional and press release claims, could apply just as easily to an organization's competitors.

Despite a common misperception, mission statements are intended to target and possibly inspire internal audiences: employees, stakeholders, boards of directors and business partners. While the purpose of mission statements may be high-minded, they are by nature never very exciting because they are inward focused. They do not create competitive positioning for an organization's image today. A mission statement is not a part of strategic communications, primarily because it does not address what's special about a particular organization versus a competitor.

On the other hand, real awareness comes from a distinctive positioning message — crafted in plain language and free of all self-promotional jargon and fluff — that stimulates a conversation and a desire to know more.

A positioning message focuses on today and, if crafted carefully, will incisively leave an audience with a clear understanding of who you are, and what is unique about your appealing business vision.

More importantly, a positioning message is a competitive differentiator that helps a customer choose you over someone else. It's a clear, plain language message — free of promotional slogans, marketing words or buzzwords — that gets to the core of what's special about an organization's products, services and worth in the marketplace. It is a pillar of strategic communications and media leadership.

Here's a story about one organization's costly struggle with a mission statement, followed by a successful course correction.

When I began advising leaders of 4-H on a major and ongoing initiative to reshape the image and brand of that national youth development organization, I walked into an environment that had only known mission statements and slogans. 4-H, like many other such groups, had changed their mission statement so often and had come up with slogans so frequently that the general, nondescript words had lost all meaning.

Incidentally, the 4-H organization had spent hundreds of thousands of dollars on research and consultants and branding experts, and all they ever ended up with were slogans. One 4-H branding campaign, developed by the Advertising Council, promoted the slogan "Are you into it?" The effort cost the youth group a fortune in advertising, and post-campaign testing revealed that it had actually damaged the reputation of the 4-H brand.

Surveys conducted before and after the campaign revealed a 10 percent drop in respect for the organization's image because of the branding effort. It was found that the "Are you into it?" phrase was so bland and nondescriptive that it painted 4-H as a boring organization with no special qualities or appeal. In other words, "Are you into it?" communicated little value and was so general sounding that it meant nothing.

Yet 4-H's struggle to find its distinctive brand identification went much deeper. On the Internet, there are more than 800 Web sites related to 4-H, and as a result, there are seemingly just about as many descriptions of 4-H. Many people know the brand and 4-H clover logo, but few have an understanding of what 4-H does as an organization. 4-H had become its own competition.

4-H leaders had invested many hours revising their mission statement, and yet they continued to fail to attract new members and funding. In fact, both were on a decline. This decline can be attributed partly to the use of a mission statement in attempts to market 4-H to new audiences. By its very nature, the statement lacked differentiating characteristics that might show exciting reasons to choose 4-H over another youth organization.

The 4-H organization simply lacked a clear, credible positioning that would provide the chance to break through clutter and recalibrate the 4-H image so it would have greater influence attracting funding, members and media coverage. 4-H needed one compelling plain language sentence that described the value of the organization to all its audiences. I call it a conversation starter because it not only captures interest in 4-H, but also creates a desire to know more.

I believed the solution could be found by talking with the youth of 4-H around America. The 4-H organization had previously spent a fortune on market research and advertising yet had *never* interviewed the number one and most important audience — the youth who belong to 4-H — to determine how they might describe the 4-H experience. Everything to that point had been from the perspective of adults, not youths. Grown-ups trying to figure out how to capture the attention of kids seldom works, as any parent knows.

My strategy was to find a way to describe the unique soul of 4-H in words that were clear, free of adjectives and left no one out. In all of 4-H's branding efforts in the past, no one had ever gone out and interviewed the young people of the organization in such a detailed manner.

As I traveled from state to state, meeting with groups of 4-H youth and listening to how they described the 4-H adventure, I heard the same words being used by many youths, whether they were in Madison, Ga., or Davis, Calif. I call those words an organization's common-thread words.

4-H youth were using common-thread words like "community" and "young people." They said they were "learning" by working together in a mentoring environment with adults. I asked what they were learning. "Leadership, citizenship and life skills," they answered.

During my interviews, I found it interesting that 4-H members often referred to their peers as "young people" as we discussed ways to describe 4-H to an outside audience. The adult leaders of the 4-H organization, by contrast, usually referred to the young people as "kids."

I listened to the youth of 4-H, and they told me, "4-H is a community of young people across America, who are learning leadership, citizenship and life skills."

The youth had defined one of the strongest positioning messages I had ever heard, and they had used distinctive words from their perspective, not from the viewpoint of adults talking about "kids."

The new positioning message said it all about America's oldest youth-development organization, and it said it in clear and strong words. It was an appealing message upon which to build a strategic communications campaign. Most of all, the message centered, for the first time ever, on the value of 4-H to young people. Previous attempts at messages had centered around the organization, which, at the end of the day, no one really cared about.

Before long, the entire organization was using the positioning message. It spread like wildfire. A young 4-H girl stood at a podium before the governor of Indiana and 300 people to dedicate remodeled 4-H buildings at the Indiana State Fair, and she began by saying, "4-H is a community of young people across America, who are learning leadership, citizenship and life skills."

The 4-H youth put it on T-shirts, Web sites and blogs. County agents used it on their e-mail signature lines. It is being used everywhere, and at most levels of the organization. And the result is that wider audiences are becoming aware of the scope and impact of 4-H today in helping America's young people.

The 4-H organization, like countless other groups, had been caught up in a recent trend to improve and boost its brand, when what it really needed was a distinctive way to describe its core value in a single sentence.

Can you describe the core value of your business, organization or product in a single sentence? Can you explain your endeavor in a few words that connect credibly with audiences that are important to you, including the news media? Is your organization speaking with a consistent "voice" that clearly and simply resonates favorably with audiences?

So many organizations hire branding firms that suggest all their problems will be solved with a new logo, slogan and letterhead. That might help, but it's not the complete solution. Reciting a slogan will never impress anyone, attract visitors to a Web site or blog, or get meaningful media attention.

A clear and compelling positioning message is essential because it sets you apart from your competitors. And here's a tip: To sharpen your appeal, narrow your position. We cannot be all things to all people, so don't try. Just be genuine and authentic. To be successful, we must focus on one thing, and be the best at it.

One thing, you say? Yes. Your organization might do many other things, but it should be recognized for excelling at one thing. Get people talking about that, and you will win competitively.

Chapter Twenty-Three:
The Price of a Forgettable Slogan

Let's take a quick look at the phenomena of slogans ... and why most fall short of achieving meaningful results in either communications or brand differentiation.

Out of full disclosure, I admit that I've never been enthusiastic over the effectiveness of using slogans as a way to build awareness or create competitive success. Slogans generally are both inappropriate and useless when seeking media coverage and building authentic trust with audiences. Like mission statements, there is little meaningful time in today's highly competitive online environment for people to be distracted by slogans when they are seeking substance.

Slogans, taglines and marketing buzzwords are, well, not useful elements of normal and effective communication among people. Some people think that slogans will catch attention, but I believe that most slogans, while sometimes clever sounding, are also forgettable. They have no place in the highly competitive style of strategic communications in today's world.

When we as human beings communicate with each other and through the media, we speak in complete sentences and thoughts, at least most of the time. Our children are an exception, of course, especially when they are teenagers.

The best way to catch someone's attention is with a straightforward, clear and plain language message that connects and resonates favorably with audiences or people you are attempting to reach and influence.

I was reading the *Washington Business Journal*, and I stopped at a story with the headline TOURISM OFFICIALS TO UNVEIL NEW D.C. "BRAND" RESEARCH. The people who run the Washington, D.C.,

Convention and Visitors Authority had conducted new research to help the nation's capital develop a new "brand." Halfway through the story was this line: "For nearly a decade, Washington, D.C., has used 'Washington, D.C.: The American Experience.'"

When I read that, my reaction ran from slight embarrassment to curiosity. I live in the Washington area, yet I was not aware of a slogan for the city that, according to the story, had been used for nearly a decade.

Not to be deterred, I Googled "The American Experience." On the first page of search results, Google listed sites related to the PBS television program of that name and to a Native American Web site, but nothing about Washington, D.C. A couple of Google pages later, I found a modest-looking and static Web site for Washington.org,[43] the self-proclaimed "official" site for tourism in the nation's capital.

Yet, and here was the really curious part, the Washington.org site failed to define the catch phrase "The American Experience" or its relevance to the nation's capital. That is a primary pitfall of relying on slogans and taglines. The words most often lack emotional and logical context. They do not make logical sense.

Still feeling a little disappointed that I was not aware of Washington's tourism slogan, I conducted a straw poll of about sixty people who all have a close connection in one way or another with the nation's capital. I e-mailed one question: "With no prompting (or Googling), can you tell me what Washington, D.C.'s tourism promotion slogan is? Yes or no."

My random survey group included newspaper reporters, people at marketing and public affairs agencies in Washington, nationally known syndicated columnists, network and local journalists and broadcasters, a few secretaries, three attorneys, a Realtor in Washington, local business owners, the leaders of trade associations and nongovernmental organizations, and some friends. Only one person knew the slogan — just one. For everyone else, including me, Washington's decade-old tourism slogan had missed us.

Now, you might respond that Washington's tourism slogan is intended for potential tourists around the country, not locals, and I would agree up to a point. But one of the easiest and most effective

---

[43] www.washington.org

ways for any organization or city to market itself is from the inside out, by getting people at home or within your organization excited first. Let the local folks (or your employees) help spread the news.

Organizations, like Washington's Convention and Visitors Authority, and major companies regularly pay hefty fees to branding firms for what might only amount to a new coat of paint, and a thin coat, at that. It's not surprising that the profit margin for client assignments at the largest branding firms often exceeds 70 percent. There is big money to be made in creating slogans.

On the other hand, many communications professionals have become skilled at developing positioning messages that help clients more clearly reposition their image and, ultimately, their brand. A brand is not bought in a contrived or forced manner but is earned through consistent words, deeds and actions that communicate authentic value.

A more effective approach in today's world, which is filled with cluttered messages, is to focus on the authentic value an organization delivers, using a few plain language words that are free of adjectives. There is no need to tell the whole story; tell just enough to give an audience, including the media, a desire to know more.

A few carefully chosen and distinctive words can work wonders to differentiate an organization from competitors, leave a favorable impression and build a distinctive brand.

Apple, the innovative company I use as an example throughout this book, created the Macintosh computer and the widely popular iPhone and iPod, among many other cool consumer products. I look at Apple because the company is one of the best examples of an organization that lives and speaks its brand image.

When you purchase any Apple product, the company backs it up with a support network, online and via telephone, that is easy to understand, even if your skills are new to the product. Apple's warranty is solutions based, not seemingly avoidance based, as with its competitors.

The Cupertino, Calif., based company is renown for reflecting its brand promise in everything it does. So, it is no surprise that Apple has made many friends, including those in mainstream and online media communities.

When Apple has good news, it is trumpeted by the media. On the other hand, when Apple has a problem, as all companies encounter, the media is often more understanding.

This isn't about having a nifty-looking Apple logo that's become somewhat of a cult symbol; it is about living the company's image and reputation in everything it does. And in the computer manufacturing industry, Apple is pretty much alone on that score.

How does Apple talk about itself to the media? With plain language words and phrases and avoiding technology jargon, as I have written earlier. There is very little self-promotional boilerplate on Apple's Web site. Small wonder that Apple's sales soar, even when the rest of the country is in a recession.

Apple's positioning statement is fluid, conversational and adaptive. Here's an example: "Apple ... reinvented the personal computer in the 1980s with the Macintosh, and today continues to lead the industry in innovation with its award-winning computers, OS X operating system, and iLife and professional applications."

The company's news releases are free of those ABOUT paragraphs that amount to little more than cheap self-promotion. Apple is one of those few companies that understands that the "about" section compromises the journalistic integrity of news releases. Besides, if someone wants more information, one can check the company's Web site.

I suppose that years as a communications strategist has taught me that slogans and taglines will never replace authentic messages that seem to reach inside and connect with our emotions and common sense.

But, while on the subject, let me share a couple of exceptions. A few slogans have endured over the years because they share the common essential element of being able to connect emotionally and logically with our primal needs or desires.

"The American Experience" failed miserably for Washington, D.C., because it lacked relevance, inspiration and meaning, and it did not reflect any true quality of contemporary Washington, D.C. Besides, PBS Television had already trademarked it.

The introduction of the 1960s Virginia Slims cigarette brand brought with it the "You've come a long way, baby" slogan, which was aimed at women. Even though cigarette advertising is now banned on television, the slogan lived on for a while in pop lexicon.

"GE brings good things to life" suggests something warm and cozy, but what does it really mean about the conglomerate that manufactures lightbulbs and jet aircraft engines and owns NBC, among other things?

I must admit that I do have a favorite slogan: "Virginia is for lovers." These four words work so well to evoke imagery and emotion because they are as much a positioning statement as a slogan. Someone can begin a media interview or make a speech by saying, "Virginia is for lovers …" and then explain why.

"Virginia is for lovers" was created by a trio of tourism and advertising pros in Richmond, Va., in 1969, and it is still recognized widely, even though there has been a movement to officially retire the words. Incidentally, there are many advertising people around the country who claim to have created the line, including one ad guy in Richmond, Va., who was a child in 1969 when the slogan debuted.

Maybe it was because the timing was right in 1969, when the slogan was launched. Even though the United States was mired in a war in Vietnam, love was in the air and a common theme — Erich Segal's book *Love Story* was a best seller, as was Jacqueline Susann's *The Love Machine*. It was the time of Woodstock, when 300,000 young people gathered for a weekend of peace, love and music.

The Virginia tourism people say that part of the mystique of the slogan is that it has meant many things to different people. It connects on an individual level. When I hear the phrase "Virginia is for lovers," it conjures up in my mind positive and nostalgic images of the state where I grew up.

On the other hand, thousands of slogans never quite work, even though organizations hire branding experts and invest significant resources.

My best advice for creating distinctive positioning for your organization is to begin crafting the story about how customers or clients benefit from the authentic value your organization delivers.

- Don't talk about yourself, because no one cares.

- Get outside of your organization and talk about the benefits and value people get from what your organization does.

- Focus on a way to begin telling your story in just a couple of clear and direct sentences.

- Get right to the point.

Remember my example earlier in this book, of the message that the youth of the national 4-H organization came up with, which said it all: "4-H is a community of young people across America who are learning leadership, citizenship and life skills." The simple sentence has worked to distinctively capture the special value of the 4-H experience for young people.

Chapter Twenty-Four:
A Handshake Rather Than E-Mail

Connecting with the world through your computer is one thing, but it's not the ultimate solution, and it never will be. Nothing beats personal contact — either a face-to-face meeting or a telephone call — with someone who is influential and who can help make a positive difference or extend the awareness and reputation of your organization.

For example, there's a technique in media relations, called a deskside briefing, for becoming acquainted with a reporter. A deskside briefing can be one of the best ways for an executive or newsmaker to generate initial interest in his or her company or organization.

Even in the digital era, it is just as valid and appropriate as always. It's particularly effective because the tactic is not widely used by many practitioners of public relations today, who strangely seem to shun any direct contact with the media. If you play your cards right and follow some basic rules, a deskside session could lead to a good story.

Before I go into the tactic any farther, I should point out that the idea of a face-to-face briefing has been dissed by a few of today's Internet-centric and, I might add, less experienced public relations people. They claim it is old school, and it might seem to be. But not everything can be achieved online or through e-mails, especially personal relationships. Just ask Sir Richard Branson of Virgin Group, Tony Hsieh of Zappos, Steve Jobs at Apple and other high profile executives who meet face-to-face or are in personal contact all the time with influential thought leaders of industry and in the media.

The approach I want to explain involves scheduling a brief, informal meeting with a reporter or blogger who covers your industry or business. The objective is to get an understanding of their needs and talk briefly about an issue that your organization is involved in. A deskside briefing is an informal way to lay the groundwork for a possible future story, provide editorial direction, establish yourself as a trusted resource and build a relationship. It is not to ask for a story.

Let's say that a few journalists have written about your company, product or service, but it would be a major coup to have a story appear in the media. Despite numerous calls by your communications people to the correct reporter, nothing is happening. It's going nowhere. Phone calls are either not being returned, or the reporter has told you that while the story seems interesting, it lacks a good news angle. That's a polite way of saying the reporter perceives your outfit as no big deal and unworthy of his or her time.

Here's how it works:

The objective is to get yourself or a leading executive at a company or organization in front of the right reporter for a brief background meeting. The deskside briefing is *not* billed as an interview but as a quick background briefing. Ideally, you should meet the reporter informally for about 20 to 30 minutes before his or her normal workday begins and — this is very important — keep the meeting shorter than the time requested.

Before attempting to schedule a deskside briefing, do some research about the reporter to make certain you are contacting the right person. Look at some of his or her recent stories so you can mention them in your conversation and compliment the reporter's work. Look for areas of overlap or connection between what this reporter has previously written and your potential story.

All reporters have a particular *beat*, or range of topics, they cover, often defined by their personal interests. For example, Thomas Friedman at the *New York Times* has become one of America's foremost opinion leaders on the Middle East because of his interest in the region; Walt Mossberg is the popular technology columnist at the *Wall Street Journal*; and Jackie Northam covers national security issues at National Public Radio. You get the picture.

Crafting an effective introductory e-mail or telephone approach to catch a reporter's attention can reach the level of a form of art. Being concise is key when it comes to asking a journalist to meet or speak by telephone, not necessarily about a possible story idea, but just for an informational briefing. You must create a concise, focused, alluring and, most of all, low-key approach in order to schedule the meeting.

Once you have the right journalist, you need to capture his or her interest, the quicker the better. Your chances diminish the more you talk. Whether you send an e-mail, leave a message on voice mail, or actually reach reporters on the phone live, get right to the point with an action plan.

Do something unusual; do not pitch or ask for a story. That's too predictable. Instead, say something like, "My purpose for contacting you is not about a story, but rather to introduce myself and my organization and share some information, which is in the industry you regularly cover."

Tell the reporter you may a possible story idea or certainly something of interest and briefly explain why you think he or she might be interested in it, referencing something similar the person has written. Play to his ego and to the areas he writes about.

You are not pitching a story but merely seeking a brief meeting or conversation to provide background and position yourself as a trusted resource. This unique approach implies exclusiveness. Underscore to the reporter that you know the importance of his work demands, for you have a limited amount of time as well, so an early morning meeting might work best. Remember, it's an informal meeting.

Here are some ground rules:

- Do not send information prior to the deskside meeting, for a couple of reasons. First, it begins to feel like a predictable story pitch. Second, you may be sending the wrong material. Third, the reporter is likely to lose or misplace the stuff sent in advance, which could create an awkward moment when you arrive and the reporter can't find it. Only send advance material if the reporter specifically requests it, and then only send what is requested — nothing more.

- Resist the traditional public relations urge to impress the reporter with reams of news media kits and a load of other stuff. When you go to a deskside briefing, intentionally take only the briefest supporting material with you, preferably no brochures and no media kit. In that way, by providing specific material the reporter wants because of the meeting or conversation, you create an opportunity for personalized follow-up contact with the reporter. That not only keeps the reporter focused on your potential story, but it also works to build a relationship of trust and confidence with the reporter, boosting your chances that a story will happen.

- Remember the purpose of the deskside briefing: It is not an interview but a briefing, and you are not asking the reporter to do a story. It's an informal chance to meet and become acquainted for the first time with a journalist who can be important to you and your organization. It is *relationship building*.

- During the meeting, focus on one or two main messages. Avoid making the reporter's eyes glaze over by talking about too many issues. The conversation is not about you but about what might interest the journalist. Focus on developing a couple of ideas that might complement the reporter's past articles.

- At the conclusion of a deskside briefing, define an informal follow-up plan. Ask the reporter you can send any material that might be helpful. Find out the best way you can stay in touch. Via e-mail? Phone?

- Treat the deskside briefing as a bonding opportunity to develop a working relationship with the journalist. Thank the reporter for his or her time. Show sincere appreciation. And never ask for a story. Even if the reporter suggests a possible story, say you would be happy if the conversation led to that, but you just appreciated chatting with him or her for a few minutes.

I once took a CEO for an early morning deskside briefing with a reporter, and when the meeting concluded, the executive could not resist the urge, even though I had cautioned him against it, to ask, "When are you going to do a story?" The reporter understandably looked ambushed and deceived, and clearly he had been by the CEO.

Most journalists have good examples of effective deskside meetings or telephone conversations. Newspaper columnist and HDNet television senior correspondent Greg Dobbs, for example, told me about a meeting he had with a public relations representative regarding the trend toward just-in-time manufacturing, a process of efficiently managing often costly inventories to allow more competitive pricing of products.

"She made me aware of a concept growing in popularity in American industry," Dobbs said. "When she had my attention, she then offered her client to serve as my example in a feature story. It worked. Win-win. She turned me on to the concept and then, by getting me in her client's door, earned her pay."

The *New York Post*'s Linda Stasi cautions, "We know and you know that you're there to sell something I probably don't want, so be up front about it. Never, never oversell or lie. If you do, remember, the reporter is the one with the last word, and that word will be in ink and read (hopefully) by many people."

A face-to-face meeting is preferable, but the concept will work just as well with a telephone conversation if distance is a challenge. A deskside briefing in whatever form it takes is a resourceful way to get the attention of an important reporter and establish a productive working relationship that will pay off and help you get an edge on your competitors.

Sometimes what may seem like a low-tech approach works best to build trusted relationships and positions you in the enviable position of becoming a resource to the media.

Chapter Twenty-Five:
Be Clever and Bold

Everyone, including journalists, enjoys imaginative new ideas that get their attention. But if your idea only distracts the recipients, or annoys them by filling their carpets with confetti, you've lost the battle.

Unfortunately, in the public relations business, which should be distinguished by clever thinking, imaginative and new ideas and approaches for effective communication are rare. The business is instead driven by the same dull, worn-out and copycat tactics over and over and over.

There is nothing wrong with trying to get the media's attention through a small gift, so long as it's relevant to the story and not something expensive enough that it might compromise integrity or the rules of a media organization. It's easy enough to find out what those rules are by making a few phone calls to reporters. Just ask.

On the other hand, there are exceptions or gray areas, I suppose, in a journalist accepting gifts during the course of doing a story. The story about Mike Wallace of *60 Minutes* and Washington, D.C., philanthropist Catherine Reynolds is an example that jumps out.

CBS news program *60 Minutes* decided to do a story about Reynolds, who had been the target of numerous local newspaper stories about her fight with the Smithsonian Institution. She admits she had caused some controversy in the musty, stodgy gentlemen's club of philanthropy in the nation's capital.

Reynolds created a fortune by turning around a failing student loan company. Then, as the head of the philanthropic Catherine B. Reynolds Foundation, she gave away millions of dollars to charities and the arts. A few years ago, Reynolds offered $38 million dollars to the Smithsonian

Institution, but when she and the Smithsonian couldn't agree on how she wanted the money to be spent, she withdrew the gift and turned her generosity toward the Kennedy Center in Washington.

Mike Wallace and a *60 Minutes* camera crew decided to follow Ms. Reynolds around for a few days and find out something about this new benefactor suddenly on the forefront of Washington society. They wanted to know what she was up to. Following her around included accompanying her on a trip to Europe aboard a luxury corporate jet she had hired.

There are still some unanswered questions about whether she and her husband would have flown in such lavish style had Wallace and his crew not been along. People close to the project have told me it was an intelligently planned setup to manipulate Wallace. But everyone flew to London aboard a Gulfstream IV business jet, and it was first-class treatment all the way for Wallace, his producer, his camera crew and a couple of public relations consultants.

And just to make sure everyone had a good time, digital cameras were among the gifts Ms. Reynolds and her husband presented the CBS News folks.

At this point, you might be wondering what kind of story the occasionally sharp-elbowed Wallace, famous for his "ambush" style of TV news, did on Reynolds. Well, it was an extremely favorable and flattering feature, nothing like all the other stories written about her. In fact, the two of them got along "fabulously," as someone close to the story shared with me, and it showed on the air.

Prior to agreeing to do the story with *60 Minutes*, Reynolds had hired a major public relations agency to frame just the right story angle, feeling and environment to win over and control *60 Minutes*' coverage, and it worked.

Let me point out that the hard-hitting days of ambush investigative journalism at *60 Minutes* ended more than two decades ago. The attack dog style tended to make viewers uncomfortable and advertisers squeamish. Mike Wallace and his pals on *60 Minutes* are more feature- and book review-oriented today ... and considerably less controversial by design in an attempt to appeal to a dwindling television audience.

Knowing Wallace's once-edgy type of reporting had softened in his senior years, the public relations experts did their homework. They skillfully crafted an approach that would play to his interest in helping the underdog.

Coached and briefed, Reynolds appeared to Wallace as a successful businessperson, which she was, who had been unfairly harassed by old guard society when she attempted to be a generous philanthropist who only wanted to help improve some of America's most respected cultural institutions. That was the tone of the story that appeared on *60 Minutes*, and the string of negative stories in the local press ended after such powerful national exposure.

Riding on the Gulfstream and receiving the nice cameras didn't hurt the news crew's opinion of Reynolds. After all, CBS could have said no to the gifts and royal treatment, in keeping with long-standing CBS corporate policy. A now-retired CBS News correspondent in Washington told me they should have said "Hell, no!" to the gifts.

On the other hand, the luxury is okay with their bosses if a news crew can make a ride on a private jet part of the story. Shooting a little snippet of video of Reynolds while in the air en route to London makes everything just fine, I suppose.

Wallace's warm and fuzzy defending of Ms. Reynolds subsequently earned him invitations to become a permanent fixture in Washington society events sponsored by the clever philanthropist. The intelligent PR people she hired effectively proved how easy it is to control the media, even a major story on *60 Minutes*. You can too.

Sir Richard Branson, the English entrepreneur and natural showman, does not need a public relations agency to create stunts that favorably boost awareness about his business endeavors. Sir Richard's skillful 2007 launch of his airline, Virgin America, into the hotly competitive, coveted and highly political U.S. air carrier territory is classic.

Branson asked TV comic and Comedy Central faux news commentator Stephen Colbert to be onboard the inaugural New York to San Francisco flight, along with a flock of beautiful women, thus generating great widespread online buzz, mainstream photo opportunities, television news coverage by numerous stations and networks, and extensive word of mouth. It was "brilliant," as my English friends say.

When I was head of global corporate communications at Gulfstream Aerospace, I always questioned the relevance and purpose of promotional materials that we gave to the news media. I never wanted to distract from a story pitch by sending anything other than background material that was focused on getting the story. I sent no extraneous gifts or trinkets that might possibly derail our goal of getting a story.

I had, however, the ultimate promotional tool at my disposal, which no one else on earth had, not even Sir Richard Branson. I had an ultra long-range Gulfstream V business jet, an aircraft that could fly higher — 50,000 feet — and farther — 6,500 nautical miles — than most other aircraft in service. It is the most elegant and certainly the sexiest business jet in the sky, a symbol of achievement and success. My responsibility was to introduce the Gulfstream V to the world and build prominent visibility to attract wealthy customers.

Gulfstream, like other business aircraft manufacturers, had previously promoted its planes in the aviation trade publications and had, as a result, gotten lost in all the competitive clutter. They had for years sent out press releases and media kits to the trades, just as everyone else was doing, and it had not moved the needle toward generating widespread media coverage. Gulfstream had never considered that they might be reaching out to the wrong audience.

I took a completely different approach and did something unheard of in the aircraft business. Corporate CEOs and wealthy individuals, the people who make the decisions and can afford to buy a $40 million Gulfstream V, don't read aviation trades. Corporate executives who want to buy a super-pricey business jet usually need approval from their board of directors. But first the executives need a story to persuade their boards. So I used online and the mainstream media, including the *Wall Street Journal*, to deliver a story. By taking the Gulfstream V before broader business audiences, we went to where the customers are, and it worked like a charm.

Snagging front-page coverage in papers from Los Angeles to Brussels to Beijing to Johannesburg required giving many free rides to many reporters. And what a perk it was! When I took the first Gulfstream V aircraft on world demo tours, I would contact feature and business reporters in advance to alert them that the Gulfstream V was coming to their town. At first, their reaction was, "So what?"

Then I would offer a brief flight that would take them up to an altitude of 50,000 feet, up above all other aircraft traffic, where the sky is nearly cobalt blue, and they could clearly see the curvature of the earth. No one declined. Then I would say that the only catch was that I hoped they would write at least part of their story while at 50,000 feet. Everyone agreed.

To contrast the exclusivity of riding aboard a Gulfstream V, I kept it simple by giving each reporter who flew with us up to 50,000 feet a top-quality blue ball cap, the same kind worn by Gulfstream's test pilots, embroidered GULFSTREAM V WORLD TOUR. Was the ball cap an imaginative idea as a gift? Well, I've seen better. Was it relative to the event? You bet! Only those people who flew on the aircraft got a cap. I know of some journalists who, years later, still covet those hats, because their owners can still boast of flying in a GV to an altitude of 50,000 feet, nearly the edge of space. It was simple, classy and relevant, and it worked.

When I pitched a *BusinessWeek* correspondent on doing a cover story about Theodore Forstmann, the investor who owned Gulfstream at the time, the part of the deal that clinched the story was a commitment to shuttle the reporter around on a Gulfstream as he gathered background for his story. The reporter actually asked for the rides to sort of … kind of … get a feel for traveling in the lap of luxury. He wanted to know what it felt like to be pampered. Forget the flight cap; the rides worked, and a favorable cover story was in the bag, guaranteed.

There is a similarity between the countless media rides that I staged aboard a new Gulfstream V with how CBS' *60 Minutes* received a first-class flight to London with Catherine B. Reynolds. I developed a strategy to build much greater global awareness in order to differentiate an expensive and special business aircraft from competitors, and to generate mainstream media coverage that was unprecedented in the business aviation industry. The goal was to sell airplanes. Ms. Reynolds used the exclusive environment within a transatlantic Gulfstream flight to establish a bond of friendship with Mike Wallace that clearly influenced his story on *60 Minutes*.

By promoting the Gulfstream V prominently with clever stories in the mainstream news media and online, while all other business aircraft companies focused entirely on the narrow reach of the aerospace industry trade publications, we were able to reposition the brand of a Gulfstream jet as the hallmark of business aviation.

It happened through a strategy of shifting corporate focus outward to emphasize the merits of Gulfstream as a corporate tool for business success. The tactic used the mainstream news media to carry the message directly to corporate executives, wealthy individuals, and important decision makers around the world. Gulfstream has become, as a result, the most prestigious ride in the sky.

The results were dramatic. Orders for the Gulfstream V jumped, sales increased by more than 400 percent, and the company went public through a highly successful oversubscribed initial public offering (IPO).

The rules and boundaries for a journalist accepting a gift are ever shifting, defined and self-imposed, also varying by each news organization. It's not determined by government regulations or mandated by industry rules. Most professional news organizations have established clear policies for their employees, which set limits on what constitutes a token gift and what is bribery or payola, and therefore forbidden. The rules vary from one news organization to another. So if you have a question about gift giving, don't assume. It's always best to ask first and avoid a possible awkward situation with a journalist.

There's nothing wrong with asking the media to sample a product or service in order to drive home a promotional message, as long as the campaign is imaginative, savvy and, most of all, relevant to the story. Sometimes you might get lucky and offer a special perk or exclusive benefit that the media can experience in the course of covering your story. You will be surprised by how that most often results in favorable media coverage.

Chapter Twenty-Six:
Ready for 15 Minutes

Much of this book has focused on communications techniques from a journalist's perspective, which will help a communications professional or media savvy leader better communicate vision and messages through the powerful conduit of the media, mainstream and online. I have written a good deal on understanding how journalists approach their jobs and what elements need to come together to create legitimate news.

If you want to achieve outstanding coverage by the media — whether a daily newspaper, cable news, blog, or online news service — it only makes sense to speak their language and understand what they need. This understanding of the media will give you a competitive edge and advantage during 15 minutes of fame, to borrow the expression coined by artist Andy Warhol.

An interview with the media can occur anytime and any place. An interview can be planned or happen spontaneously, with or without warning. An interview may result because you have contacted someone with a good, timely story idea, or because the telephone rings, and a reporter at the other end of the line is asking for just a few minutes of your time to answer some questions.

Either way, the primary objective of effective strategic communications is to communicate the story you want to tell as clearly, openly and accurately as possible, in a controlled way, which helps ensure a good image and reputation for you or your organization.

The job of a reporter is to ferret out a story that will be of interest to readers, listeners or viewers. With so many mainstream daily newspapers on the financial ropes and struggling against odds for survival, we see a few writers overstepping accepted standards of journalism to become more sensational in their stories. It is merely a foolish attempt to attract readers who are no longer reading newspapers because they have flocked online. But we need to be mindful nonetheless.

An interview is not a conversation. It is a ritual in which the reporter seeks a news story, sometimes based on a preconceived notion, and you deliver focused messages that credibly tell your story. You want good coverage; the reporter wants news. Remember, it's not a conversation.

A few rules: Never guess when you don't know. Always tell the truth. Know when to stop talking, especially about issues outside your area of expertise. It's also important to know when to keep quiet and listen.

Never permit an attorney to write your talking points. Few lawyers know anything about the skill of transparent communications and will actually create problems by saying too much, too little or responding to a question that was not asked.

The lesson is to limit your area of expertise and remember a quote often attributed to Grover Cleveland, the former president of the United States, who allegedly said, "I never got in trouble with things I didn't say." Incidentally, it is nearly impossible to confirm whether Cleveland actually said that or whether it is myth. Regardless, it is a good adage to remember.

Here's a list of interview dos and don'ts that I have observed from many years as a network news correspondent and then as a strategic communications agency executive. The list has changed many times to adapt to the changing techniques of the media, mainstream and online. But the premise is grounded always in accuracy, openness and transparency. No one will ever fault you for telling the truth.

First, the things you can do in an interview:

- *Always remember: It's your agenda.* You do an interview not to help a reporter but to communicate a clear message or image; you become the face of your organization in an interview. Set your own boundaries. If a reporter calls unexpectedly for an interview, you are under no obligation to drop everything and give an interview at that moment, as I mentioned earlier. Explain that you are finishing something and will call the reporter back in a few minutes, perhaps up to an hour. Ask about the subject he or she wants to discuss. Then take quality time to focus on what you want to say. The extra time will also help settle nerves that many people experience when contacted by the news media.

- *Always think three.* Think of three messages you want to communicate in the interview. Think of how to deliver each message in an interesting, genuine and concise way. The messages are the core of what you want to communicate in the interview so stick to them. Memorize them. By having three messages, you can enhance control of an interview by providing depth and perspective. Provide examples for greater understand and to develop an interesting story.

- *Always seek opportunities to bridge to your three messages.* A *bridge* is an interview tactic to control and redirect an interview back to the subject that you want to talk about. If the reporter asks a question, for example, that is far afield from what you want to talk about, no problem. Acknowledge the reporter by answering the question briefly and then bridge back to what you want to say. A bridge can be just several words, such as, "I believe one of the most important things to remember is …" or, "We need to keep in mind that …" And then get back on track with your messages. Remember, it's your interview so make the most of it.

- *Always anticipate all questions.* When you know in advance that a reporter is doing an interview, you can do quick online research on other stories the reporter has written and can get a good feel for what questions will be asked. Never go into an interview without first making a list of questions, even tough questions, that you anticipate a reporter might ask. Ask colleagues to join in this exercise if possible. It's a good way to rehearse quickly what you might say in an interview.

- *Always know when to stop.* The best answer to a reporter's question is a clear and concise answer. The shorter the answer, the better. Hundreds of times I have heard a reporter ask a question that deserves just a 30-second response but receives a 10-minute answer, making the reporter's eyes glaze over. If a reporter thinks your answer is too short, he or she can always ask a follow-up question.

- *Always answer the question you were asked.* Listen to each question. Answer that question. Interviews are stressful enough without attempting to guess, interpret or analyze what you think the reporter's motives might be. If you don't like the direction of a question, answer it briefly and to the best of your ability, and then bridge or transition back to your own talking points, to what you want to say.

- *Always try to use quotable quotes.* Use colloquialisms, quote someone famous or use a memorable play on words, if appropriate, to make your point. Reporters love such quotable quotes. Clever or interesting quotes can make you look good in an interview and control the direction of the story.

- *Always back up message points with statistics and facts.* When you use credible data or helpful resource background to make your point in an interview, you earn respect and credibility.

- *Always remember that how you say it is as important as what you say.* In an interview, be genuine and sincere. Take some time before an interview to, as they say, get yourself in a good place. Go into an interview with a positive frame of mind. Don't be afraid to smile. Use your voice, eyes and expressions to show passion in your words, even if the interview is by telephone.

- *Always maintain eye contact.* Always look at the reporter, never allowing your eyes to stray. Eye contact tells a reporter that this interview is the most important thing you are doing right now. If your eyes wander during a television interview, the perception may be that you are nervous.

- *Always remember that a microphone is always on.* Never say anything silly or inappropriate, assuming a microphone has been switched off. It can happen to anyone. Back in the 1980s, then-president Ronald Reagan, an old pro with the media, who should have known better, jokingly said, "We begin bombing Russia in five minutes." A microphone was on, and

Reagan's playful remark made embarrassing headlines around the world. Reagan's words can be heard today on YouTube.

- *Always briefly summarize your key points at the end of the interview.* You have the forum, the spotlight, so make the most of it. A summary provides you with a final opportunity to deliver your three messages again.

Now for a short list of things to avoid doing in an interview:

- *Never say anything you don't want to see in print or hear on the air.* If you are angry with someone or a situation, don't use the interview as a forum to say something casually, on the side, that you don't think a reporter will hear or use. An interview is not a time to kid around.

- *Never take it personally or get defensive.* Reporters, in most cases, are just out doing their job of finding news stories. Work with them and everyone wins. The days of ambush journalism ended years ago.

- *Never assume an interview is a conversation.* There is nothing casual or chatty about an interview, no matter how informal a particular reporter's style might be. A reporter is always working to find a good story.

- *Never make up answers.* If you don't know, say so and promise to get the information and respond promptly.

Some people and attorneys incorrectly view the media as an irresponsible lynch mob, out to misquote and concoct inaccurate stories. That has never been my experience. On the contrary, when someone claims he or she has been misquoted in an interview, it's most often because of something the interviewee inadvertently said, or the manner in which he said it.

Misquotes usually happen because the person being interviewed has said something untruthful, contradictory or ambiguous, even though the journalist usually and wrongfully gets the blame. It happens often, however, because the interviewee simply talked too much.

Chapter Twenty-Seven:
The Camera Never Blinks

The latest video and online technology has created opportunities for doing live TV interviews from remote locations, including from your own office. It has led to an effective method for quickly getting exposure on television news programs.

For corporate, nonprofit and academic organizations that do frequent live TV appearances, it is no longer necessary for an expert spokesperson to take valuable time to travel to TV studios. VideoLink[44] is a Boston-based company that connects a growing list of clients with the TV news media by providing remotely controlled broadcast-quality cameras and all the support necessary for an organization to increase its television exposure.

It's a popular trend, particularly among cable television news programs, where producers, under tight budgets, now have a way to get timely and relevant interviews with experts at little or no cost, and with little advance notice.

Here's the important part: This is a way for any company or organization to become an active and influential participant in television media and achieve consistently favorable exposure through an endless string of interviews. The public relations teams at organizations that use the in-house TV cameras work nonstop to pitch expert spokespersons to television news programs, and it works.

VideoLink's blue-ribbon list of clients includes policy institutes, medical centers, major corporations, political groups, universities, investment banking firms, pharmaceutical companies and research organizations. Even Sir Richard Branson, billionaire entrepreneur and

---

[44] www.videolink.tv

chief of the Virgin Group, has installed a VideoLink camera at his island retreat in the British Virgin Islands as a fast and efficient method of getting his face and voice on television when news happens that might involve his business empire.

The use of VideoLink's remote cameras is so easy that it is has become commonplace by nearly every television news organization, from PBS *NewsHour* to CNN, BBC, Fox News and MSNBC.

With the proliferation of such remote telecasts come a few pitfalls, but significant opportunities as well. A downside is that there is rarely a producer or communications professional to provide last minute coaching. For example, your style of clothing, posture, expressions and hand gestures is nearly as important as what you have to say. Appearance helps convey trust and credibility.

- Look straight into the camera lens because that's where the audience is watching you. It may seem a little strange at first to get the hang of it, but if your eyes dart around the room as you speak, the audience may perceive you as shifty, nervous or uncertain of your words.

- Lean forward slightly to emphasize body language that shows you are interested and engaged in providing honest and transparent answers. People who slouch back in their chairs during interviews can send a signal, right or wrong, of arrogance.

- Avoid swiveling in the chair, even slightly, because it might make you look nervous or uncomfortable.

- Wear clothes that will not distract people from what you are saying; fairly conservative business attire in mostly solid colors is often most appropriate. Incidentally, because of today's high-quality cameras, men no longer need to wear blue shirts for TV interviews.

- If being interviewed while standing, stand up straight. Slouching can send a message of boredom or having a negative attitude.

- It's helpful to learn something about TV makeup in case the people interviewing you don't have someone there to powder your nose or forehead.

- Avoid waving your hands around during a television interview. It's distracting and might make you appear like someone in a used-car commercial or one of today's crop of overly dramatic TV reporters. If you want to make a point with hand gestures, do so with one hand, using only in meaningful movements.

- Look natural and friendly, but don't smile at the interviewer while you're talking about something serious.

I have coached newsmakers and guided them with these simple rules when facing cameras and microphones, often during impromptu and high-pressure situations. The ability to master the protocol of broadcast interviews has allowed them to focus on their words and messages they want to deliver. The resulting credibility has helped build many enduring relationships with journalists.

Lastly, if you are ambushed by a surprise question, heed the advice of the late Secretary of Defense Robert S. McNamara: Follow your best instincts and rely on the main points you want to communication in an interview. Answer the question you *wish* had been asked, so long as it is truthful.

Chapter Twenty-Eight:
Core Values and Clear Vision

When actor Rainn Wilson wanted to find a way to introduce Soul Pancake,[45] his new spiritually based social media Web site, he signed up on Twitter, joined in the discussions and attracted more than a million followers within six months. Twitter fans around the world all of a sudden had instant, interactive access to a top star of NBC's popular television program *The Office*, and he openly "tweeted" about his new online endeavor and got into online conversations with his fans.

Unlike other celebrities, Wilson smartly left open the direct message feature of Twitter, allowing fans and friends to send him personal messages. Wilson readily responded to many, often using a Twitter application on his iPhone. That small gesture of accessibility greatly enhanced his online credibility and reputation for transparency and openness.

For Wilson, bringing his motion picture and television celebrity to Twitter dramatically boosted awareness about Soul Pancake, making the Web site even more successful. Each time Wilson acknowledged a message from a follower or reposted — "retweeted" — someone's mini-post on Twitter, he knew he was making even more friends who might spread the word about Soul Pancake. It worked as a win-win for everyone: Wilson, Soul Pancake, and Wilson's fans and Twitter followers.

Every day, people in all walks of life, from movie stars and CEOs to members of the media and ordinary people, are using Twitter and other forms of online social media to discuss, share, announce something new or just to listen. It is the ultimate level playing field and is fair to all.

---

[45] www.soulpancake.com

Tony Hsieh is also quite a success story in the online world. While attending Harvard in the early 1990s, Hsieh earned money by selling pizzas. Then he got an idea for an online advertising company, and he eventually sold the company to Microsoft for $265 million.

In 1999, Hsieh became involved in a concept that would revolutionize how shoes are sold, using the Internet. The company is called Zappos,[46] a derivation of the word *zapatos*, which is Spanish for shoes.

Part of the reason for Zappos' meteoric success is that it got the economics and operations right. The company offers customers a huge selection of inventory — four million pairs of shoes (and other items, such as handbags and apparel) — which is housed in a warehouse in Kentucky next to a UPS shipping hub. Furthermore, Zappos offers free delivery ... and free return if you don't like the shoes.

Zappos has grown to more than 1,400 employees, roughly half at corporate headquarters near Las Vegas, Nev., and the other half in Kentucky; has been recognized as one of the best companies in America to work for; and, with more than ten million customers, sells more shoes than any other company on the planet.

Zappos has become a billion dollar business, and much of it has been done online, from taking orders and customer service to Hsieh having daily conversations with his customers through his CEO blog and on Twitter.

Hsieh has used the Internet not only to connect with his public and customers, but also to drive broad awareness. Sure, there has been tons of mainstream and online media coverage about Hsieh and Zappos — from Oprah and *60 Minutes* to *BusinessWeek* — yet the catalyst that caught everyone's attention was how Hsieh communicated his authentic, sincere and open style online.

Early on, Hsieh recognized the importance of investing time personally to establish and build relationships with everyone from customers and employees to reporters and people who are just curious and in the process. He is respected as a business entrepreneur and thought leader who is accessible through his blog, personal e-mail and online social media sites, such as Twitter. I caught up with him via a series of e-mails for an online interview.

---

[46] www.zappos.com

When I asked Hsieh to name the three most important elements of business in the digital age, he responded, "I would boil it down to just one thing: Embrace transparency."

"With the digital revolution," Hsieh e-scribbled, "all companies are becoming more transparent, whether they like it or not. The ones that choose to embrace transparency will be the ones that gain more trust with their employees and customers, and those are the ones that are much more likely to be successful in the long term."

Aside from his being a smart visionary with a keen sense for the online environment, I asked what made him see the importance of connecting with audiences through social media.

"At Zappos, our number one priority is our company culture," says Hsieh. "Our belief is that if we get the culture right, most of the other stuff, like delivery, great customer service and building a long-term enduring brand, will happen naturally, on its own."

"Could the Zappos business model be transplanted to revitalize such old institutions as General Motors or Amtrak?" I asked. "In other words, could the Zappos magic be cloned successfully?"

"I don't think the Zappos culture can be or should be cloned, but I do think the idea of being transparent and running a business based on core values and a meaningful vision that's not just about money and profits can work for any organization," he said. "It doesn't really matter what the core values are, as long as the entire organization commits to those core values. The most important thing in any large organization is alignment [around values and vision]."

His company's 10 core values are short, direct and posted online, naturally, for everyone to see. The core values deliver power through simplicity and clarity:

1. Deliver "wow" through service.

2. Embrace and drive change.

3. Create fun and a little weirdness.

4. Be adventurous, creative and open-minded.

5. Pursue growth and learning.

6. Build open and honest relationships with communication.

7. Build a positive team and family spirit.
8. Do more with less.
9. Be passionate and determined.
10. Be humble.

These are not core values that a management committee, badgered by someone in human resources, labored for days to develop, as is often the case at most organizations. There's consensus among the people at Zappos about these ten values. They believe in the meaning of these values, and they live them at work.

Continuing with our interview, I asked Hsieh why most companies and organizations are slow to embrace the new online world as a way to connect with and engage audiences, preferring instead to continue using Web sites to sell, market and promote in a one-way manner.

"I think it's because there's a disconnect between the internal culture of the organization, and the core values and image that the organization wants to project. It used to be that it was okay, and perhaps even expected, that a company's culture and brand were not in sync. I think we're entering an era where a company's culture and a company's brand are really just two sides of the same coin," Hsieh responded.

Then the CEO of the world's largest online shoe store turned the reality of the entire concept of public relations upside down:

> *PR used to be about who you say you are. I think today it's much more important to focus on who you are rather than who you say you are, and that really just comes down to whether every employee is committing to and living the core values of the organization.*

When you think about it in the reality of today's online digital environment, Hsieh's insight is almost like holding a mirror up to the traditional public relations business as it's been known for decades, and seeing nothing but a vanishing ghost of things past.

Times have changed. The world has changed. Styles have changed. The Internet came along and matured as the world's most powerful of communications. As the Internet's influence has grown, so too has a need for enhanced clarity, openness, credibility and collaboration.

The whole manner by which we communicate, share and exchange news, ideas and information has been altered. We build trust when we connect in terms that are timely and relevant. But we must earn trust too. We must listen, join conversations and be mindful of protocols.

As I said at the beginning, audiences do not care to hear an organization talk about itself. People only want to know how an organization's products or services benefit them and bring value to their lives.

It's all happened while mainstream media and the public relations industries were dozing.

As I said earlier, today's professional communicators must learn how to skillfully balance on lily pads in order to merge — in open, transparent and meaningful ways — the communications disciplines we have always known, together with the exciting online world in this digital era.